Museum of Thrown Objects

To Carla,

So wonderful to meet you! Loved you work — lets keep in touch!

Andrew K. Peterson

BlazeVOX [books]

Buffalo, New York

publisher of weird little books

BlazeVOX [books]

blazevox.org

2   4   6   8   0   9   7   5   3   1

B   X

Acknowledgments.

Thank you to the editors and publishers of the small presses and journals where some of these poems first appeared: *350 Poems, The American Drivel Review, Bimbo Gun, Bombay Gin, Fact-Simile, Hot Whiskey Magazine* and *Hot Whiskey Presents: The Meat Issue,* House Press *(Drill, Spell,* and *string of small machines), Matter, Pinstripe Fedora, small town, Slumgullion Magazine,* and *Transmission.*

Special thanks to Nathan Child for Photoshop assistance.

"Forged Selves (The Bjorlings)": methodological transliterations of poems by Swedish poet Gunnar Bjorling.

"The Edies": *In Memoriam* Edith Nelson, great aunt. Photographs from her personal collection are source material and inspiration.

Contents

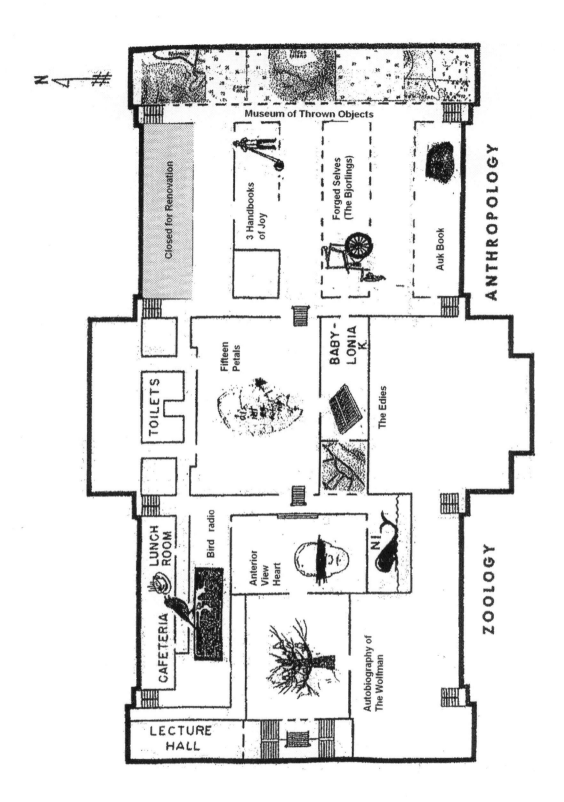

N

ANTHROPOLOGY

ZOOLOGY

Museum of Thrown Objects

Closed for Renovation

3 Handbooks
of Joy

Forged Selves
(The Bjorlings)

Auk Book

TOILETS

Fifteen
Petals

BABY-
LONIA
K.

The Edies

LUNCH
ROOM

Bird radio

CAFETERIA

Anterior
View
Heart

NI

Autobiography of
The Wolfman

LECTURE
HALL

ROUND FLOOR

For Jared Hayes

Museum of
Thrown Objects

Fifteen Petals.

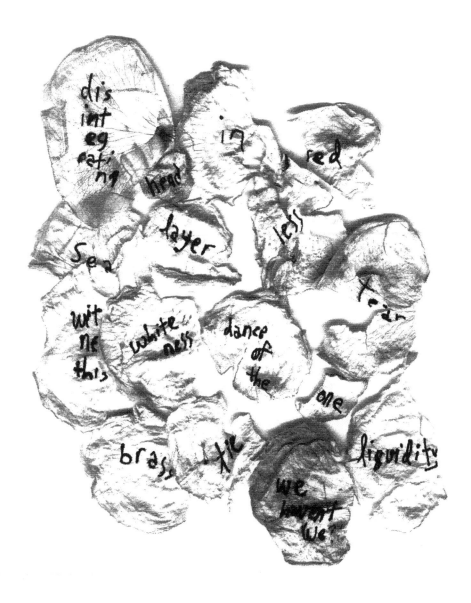

The sea: cold with white petals. We walk beside the pier on dusk's august air. From the faraway city's orange silhouette, a Haitian fight song furrows each east-faced window. This lust: otherworldly. Your miniature schnauzer loosens her leash & clouds loosen themselves from the vague green sky. She bounds toward a gathering of gulls that surround a dead trout. Gives you chase into a blur-blur among that dirty, feathered pool. With the lesson you have taught me I sit on a wet bench atop a pile of news.

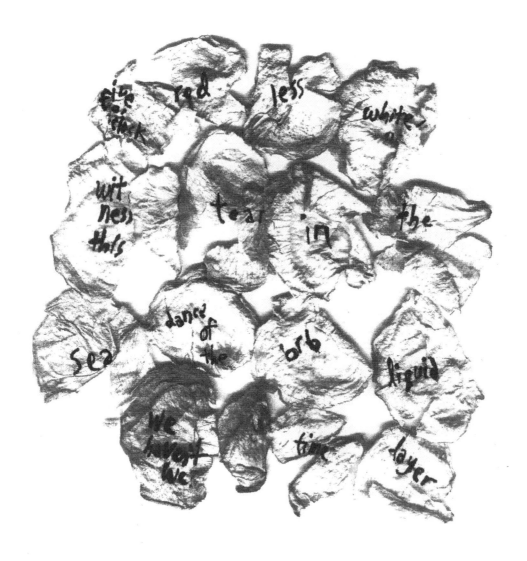

Roses beach themselves & newspapers turn into a disheveled man. The birds disperse & carry you away in their aching beaks. One rough gull remains – in turn – swallows your dog whole. You write a message in the sky with a petal-trail of birds. The disheveled man has become Jack Spicer & your dog is wrestling inside Spicer's seagull...

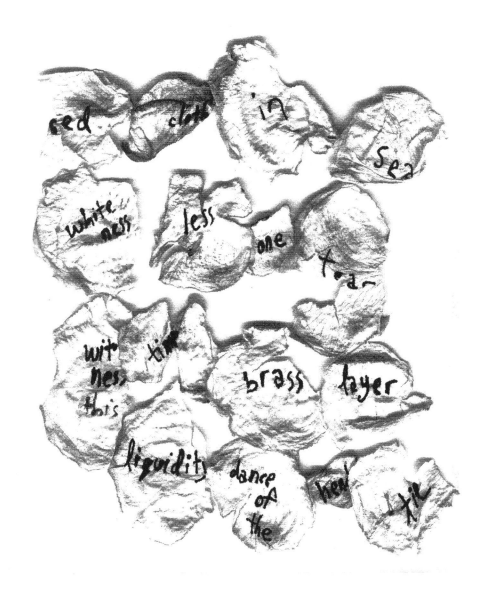

Jack Spicer covered in white petals: "You should know that gull is not mine. The rules of evidence need not apply." "And the sea?" "The sea is not mine. The sea is yours." "These petals?" "These petals are mine. I've been receiving unidentified calls all day."

A few circuit lights blink across the company switchboard. He takes petals from roughened skin & pins to my hair, my arms & calves. A green wave destroys the pier. Only your message remains…

Finishing your thought among a swirling school of live mackerel places the white surface in our palms & disappears. We are left to our bottomless sea-palms fishing these over-flowered waters...

Bird.radio

for Elizabeth Guthrie

Problems

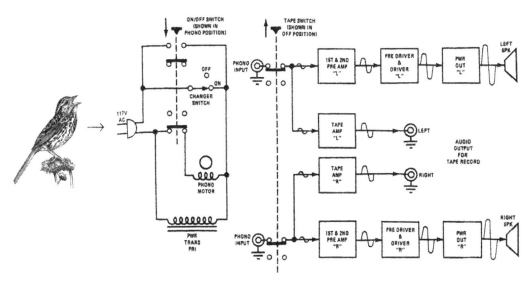

Fig. 23-40. Help! The sparrow's flown into the old Grundig! Will she ever sing again? Navigate the spectrum without a frequent loss of frequency. Guide us through this circuitry to help find her voice.

ANSWER: 87.7, *The Wren;* 88.5, *The Cardinal;* 88.9, *The Raven;* 89.3, *The Chickadee;* 90.1, *The Thrush;* 91.5, *The Thrasher;* 92.5, *The Gray Jay;* 93.3, *The Towhee;* 94.7, *The Seagull;* 95.7, *The Robin;* 96.1, *The Auk;* 97.3, *The Hawk;* 97.5, *The Blue Jay;* 98.5, *The Bellbird;* 99.1, *The Dove;* 99.5, *The Finch;* 99.9, *The Nuthatch;* 100.3, *The Hummingbird;* 100.7, *The Woodcock;* 101.1, *The Owl;* 101.7, *The Blackbird;* 102.3, *The Phoebe;* 102.5, *The Falcon;* 103.1, *The Warbler;* 103.5, *The Flicker;* 104.1, *The Whippoorwill;* 105.1, *The Crow;* 105.5, *The Canary;* 105.9, *The Albatross;* 106.7, *The Mockingbird;* 107.9, *The Bachman's Sparrow.*

87.7   *The Wren*

Beethoven's birthday, played: "Overture
for the Creature of Prometheus"

Read Ted's "Train Ride"
& when reach myself to
touch it's you I think.
                    So many blue
shades on this endless sphere.

Wrapped
inside strange slow vessels, open horns
cross in dry air "It's hard to write

for cello; so easily drowned by a key
            -board"

in the chirping circuitry, balanced
parallel rails. Horizon trick bends
steel   paths together dis-

appearing, reappearing into the next
opening   dug out, I think spring

                    *

89.3   *The Chickadee*

In the fields stands a
birch
– below
it: you – this hush

Brands us. Only thin bands
receive codes sent. New–
ly felled yellows. Signs
our names in air-
waves, vein-stems. Soft

Cusp. To fall,
it falls. receiving? Pressed
wood, it saves me from this
Time, this cumber-
some noise. In–

deed, we breathe it
in, ask nothing, note

Only that it sends —

                    *

91.5   *The Thrasher*

"Nameless now, yet sullen
ain't an option."

Back from Mozart's dire trip
to Paris, composes dirge for duo

Tree shimmers en harm-
onium, gestures intimate
with common pins, quills.

Pulls first-half-of-the-kiss
to day's sweet fugue: orange

cloud, dawn's mist-
buttoned button.

Voices, amulets of nectar
spill through the keyless locks.

White chirps against reddening
empties in   occupied room

                    *

93.3   *The Towhee*

Some faulty inner
conductor's stranded wire
static
scatters this mess-

age. Paths the blunt
breaths, pages' mute

role: barely straight,
not widely
sung. Yet if sing over

all that lasts   swallow
something tender

quarter's a sharp connector –
we may matter, our

air in mind sings ever
so sound

                    *

Open: bird chirp circuit

      price rip rich crimp put
      birch drip trick cramp rid
      bid bit pitch but preach rib
      suds song suture trip suit ditch
      perch patch heard cut dutch
      turd hit twerp curt butt
      rut perk tarp purple dub
      blue circle red bud curb
      crew wreck clip beard butch

                    *

96.1   *The Osprey*

      Interrupts the take,
      makes smile at,
      who
      to sign for the gift –
      who sent what to
      whom? Musics in his
      that, kept under his hat.
      A lovely
           loud that
      in the *that*
      that *is* is now there

                    *

97.9   *The Phoenix*
       after Zukofsky

O   pe   n, o   fie   rc   e fl
   ami   ng pi   t!
Son   g runs o   ut o f
    V   oi   ces, ou   t of   son   g,
      n   eve   r a m   emo   ry re   mains.

Wo   rds   ra   l
                        n   gin   g   fo   rms
by t   ree-l   I   g   ht. A sun—
to w   ha   t   dis   ti   ncti
                on—
        sha   d   ow spo   ke:

"Words, words, we are
words,   bi   rds, feat
            hers,
ru   dders, tur   ds." Lig
            hts in
ear   th, in   a   ir, on ea
            rth

H   ow e   lse l   ov
            e's appro   x   l   mat   e
dis   tan   ce? Gra   nt us   th   e peo
        ple's   pea   ce: her lo   ve un   hur   t, ha
        ppy   in a   ll h   ono   r. T   he im   age:

s thee so   l   ove   -d

                        *

101.1   The Owl

        "Ears" – where first heard "The Moon
        is There, I am here."

        One bludgeoned six
        AM – static – moves to fold

        clothes – instead, –
        spoon the radio for hours –

        so it sings – against me:
        "come on baby
        "come on

        "baby all I really
        "want is your love
        "then I will

        "know then I will
        "know

23

"the nearness of you

          *

101.3   *The Loon*

        mostly the male birdsongs we know
        in love but She sings also

        Everything possible floats on
        columnular
        air shimmers in
        dusk's wet net

        from the carnivorous tree –
        sorry, *coniferous* –
        from the coniferous american
        bent a lowly
        string, ask your tune to
        wail a loon with me

        solo jumps back twenty
        years. Cootie Williams alto
        growl obligato bumps
        where Wild
        Bill Davidson began
        six strings scratch OOF!!
        Wait for Art
        Blakey's moan. Now it's Lady
        Day! Drive it like you stole it, mum!
        Northbound static, dizzy loonsway

          *

103.1 *The Warbler*

        low sweet chords eyes bright mal-
        contextual arms of a new ice
        moon in charge – birds, firewood – awake

        the golden phrase   cut up   you
        want meaning I want car cr-
        ashes of monk & scrivener

        burning both ways in the current
        flows across surface of skin in
        strings in echoes thick in flowers

wrapped in copper wire. Grabbing there,
bruising whatever care — whatever small
change — disperses remnants of never-

opened stars: Hey
can you get me in for free?

*

103.3 *The Thrush*

to drip into perfect
pitch — not a crimp

in songs blue rib
above a mud, love is

sung be-
yond a yellow perch

cut from circuits
of the birch. circuit

purple, circ-
uitous rest. purple

bird beard suits
a thrush trip brap

*

103.5   *The Flicker*

we pass thru o rough strewn
nights   reroute silence

*whoever speaks is ready to
forward the affliction.* we have
this way   about us

untuned room pulled
close, circuit-

blind. Meaning, come
back to thee — door

slams open, hoping

simple so

*

104.7   *The Eagle*

if-frequencies
what holds
us together
like matter, then

Topeka is
heaven, carried
there by
an eagle, bound

pages for wings
with light water-
mark seal: ship's
wheel captures by

fire. The wind
bleating its blunt
fleece against
feather's

reddened
edges – rudder
swung off
off-course

*

Static: Organ, owl, clock

[Window, clock, organ, owl
[Organ, owl, organ
[Owl, owl, organ
[Organ, clock
[Owl, owl, organ, owl, clock
[Organ, owl, owl, clock, organ
[Organ, organ, organ, organ, organ
[Organ, owl, clock
[Organ, clock, organ, organ, window
[Window, organ, lamp, window, owl
[Owl, owl, owl, fire, organ
[Organ, window, window, organ, owl
[Owl, organ, lamp, clock, clock
[Organ, organ, window

[Organ, window, clock
[Organ, owl, owl, window, clock
[Organ, organ, organ, fire, window
[Window, organ, owl, owl
[Owl, owl, clock

*

105.1   *The Crow*

pink in bloom, winter ghost re
sumes an open circuit round all

why shouldn't they be comfy in
morning kicking icicles,

o you skiff to currants, who keels
to no one in oscillating buzz.

Who would keep
on retracing gods of

cool john floors, after
the war, I find: you write

"I don't want to go
home in December."

held together with
tape & staples. Soft & slow

pushed on & pinning a high pass
above fields of wheels & magnets

*

105.9   *The Albatross*

Commuter's dream:
              room rises
Easy to climb about
              the slow
Ceiling. If it's lost,
              it's a song
Between what I
              know, what
I don't. Do you come
              by the light
You room in, ticking

27

off numbers, foot-
Of-the-stage
my hands
Surrender, eager, like
a bell

*

106.3   *The Oriole*

In branches of sleep you
"Is that ok?"

Twinned in leaves, night's
ratty crack. drums

our grace loose in swift
times – "oh wisest of lit-

tle dogs" Orange
cloud, room floods

Orioles in, ceremonious
we wake   make dream's

stables luminous. Love
rattles in lamp's wetness

"Warbles as she flies"
Calm com-

motions. Magnet of air
Knots my time to the hook

of your kiss. Everything we need
we have right here

*

107.9   *The Bachman's Sparrow*

A beak
bursts thru
thrushes inte-
grated morning

circuits. Swoops
its brush, new shrub-
-of-a-voice lodged

in throat. Lozenge-seed

sewn clear. Closer in two
distant voices
heard thru, a better

letter than two
touched bodies un-
touched a thought of one

A Handbook of Joy

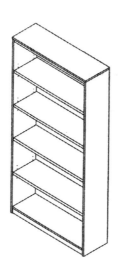

Notes on Deconstruction
After Bernard Tschumi

*"To really appreciate architecture,
you may need to commit murder."*

Remove the head of brow
& bead
of hair - black
& ochre eyes
of fuzz above
the lips
you slip
between

Tunnel the ear
& swim to peel
the mask from
the mask
from the mask from
the screw
construct of self
from shelves
& once removed
the many-selves
abandoned on hooks

& what is found:
marble
spheric smooth
head of tooth

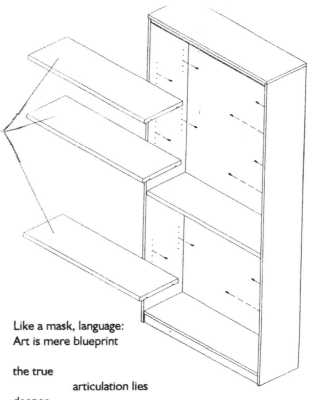

Like a mask, language:
Art is mere blueprint

the true
        articulation lies
deeper
        than this
paper-space

Remove: Mask of quietude Masque of mystery Masque intelligence
Masque deception Masque performance
Mask of reason Masque illumin
Masque dramadic Masque trauma Masque of stone
Masque seduction Masque illusion Masque of artist Masque of strange
Masque of smartest Mask of age
Masque of cellophane Mask of wound
Mask of i & l & thirdly, eye

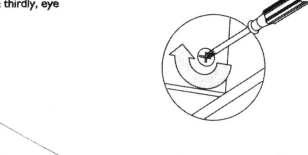

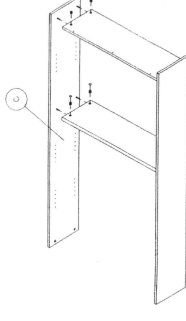

Wake!
Wrest the nude
Drawings from a pale wall:
Charcoal breasts
& chiseled bone-curve;
Do not deny the work
of art is you.

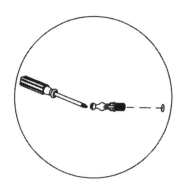

Touch the wall. You may hear
an echo. Capture in a fruit jar.

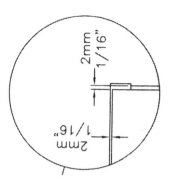

2mm
1/16"

2mm
1/16"

Knot the heat of lips common among lovers
Knot your faded words inked on bed-sheets
Knot your arm which is a rusted tool
Knot the watch that reads "medium o'clock"
Knot the stain of a living thing worse than blood
Knot your veil & wring out tangle-dream
Knot your customs stronger than love
Knot the wall which is fragment of all
Knot the breath to keep warm

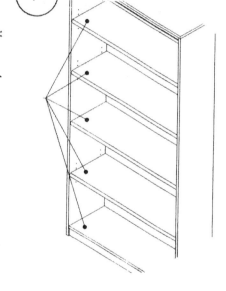

& on this movable shelf, stack:
your scent of ancient seer
your smell of criminal
your scent of dogma – copper
your smell of rotting banana
your scent of fur
your smell of flu
your scent of succumb
your smell of succor
your scent of sycamore
your smell of drunkenness
your scent of lie
your smell of hair
your scent of fungus

Flush.

 Between layers
of masque
there may be
a space-corridor:
Erebus!
Drill here.

Uncork the ceiling
& in its' place
articulate

a feeling.
Paint red if
Desire is so
colored

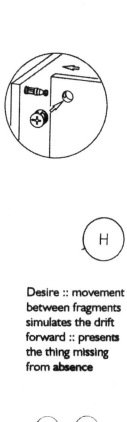

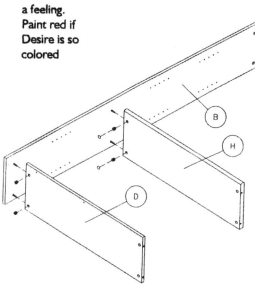

H

Desire :: movement
between fragments
simulates the drift
forward :: presents
the thing missing
from **absence**

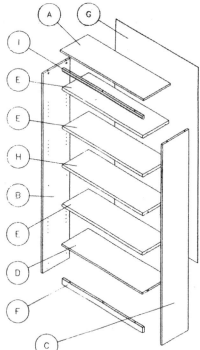

I

Once broken
down the Elemental
Growth
remains & here,
the real work
begins.

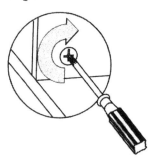

SCORE A SONG WITH ALBATROSS.

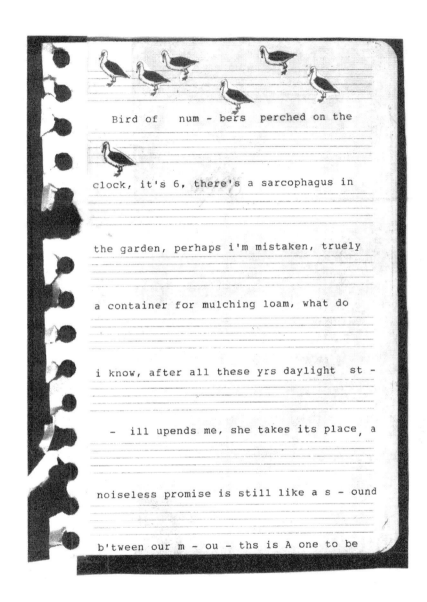

Bird of   num - bers   perched on the

clock, it's 6, there's a sarcophagus in

the garden, perhaps i'm mistaken, truely

a container for mulching loam, what do

i know, after all these yrs daylight st -

- ill upends me, she takes its place, a

noiseless promise is still like a s - ound

b'tween our m - ou - ths is A one to be

The Amateur Wind

connects us.
everything's up In.
the air a violinist.
In a cafe shape,
shifts positions. A bow.
woho us passers
By the blond-limb'd shore
shares a velvet's depth.

zCadaMEya mADa rUDaa frEna frIya dEEya ban a tO
tia AA pA chit a cada Plaud bRIA. Bon dIAm ad cITA.
BhAGat bhA gaT riTZ Itma dHALLa RA. OVEE IEE
iRT Ra Rita Rita nIdeEt bOOnHCet mrEEt YA pOntA
Cita Po nIrat pEEt acLO dREEd VA deB. Ra dA pEEcra
tAt a tA yA ya. QUA drAbrACAn Da bABbra dOk
nNNa ba cOSTAr tObra vOSS tOOSt vOSt dOBro. Co
oo noOt to WO shunGGT. xEX TRIsta squISt vISTra. No
bAUm. To NAUbrum. IFT Khtes toobrOO thrAW toOOg
bruM Toog, oOD yoOT. Habe haBUMsCraid traDUM
stRAyfum tUn taY veRM tAtum gOr Rog Mog PoJ.
DyKnw Ya brIa Sia. Mi do rEh? Dia? Xtro Xestro
Destro Xschtri Nnn. XesSu Sesu seDu xsCHru Ze.
DZEstrs. Cus XSSscze. zEZX et. ZWDd dit. XXXtig.
XiGGret ZoGOBobo prAGma mADAdad a goOWwwowo.
OnnO pAWW paNT AW. ChATch majoO casHU zIg gUMba
pIch aCKo hOho.

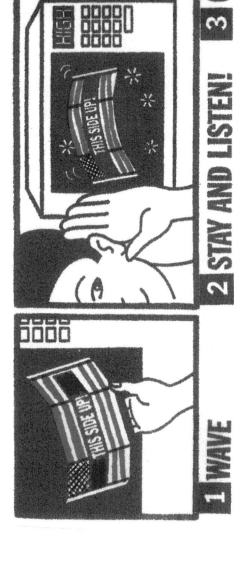

1 WAVE

My the mind a crumpled sail.

Another in the loss column.
Guarantees sixth straight losing season.

A most indignant oxygen.

The red, red

Rose must be a communist.

Torn strips of bed sheets a kind of flag.
1.2.3.4.5.6.7.

Arms a loosely wrapped coil of beaten stars.

Went back for nine seconds.

Far off, the city's orange silhouette.

2 STAY AND LISTEN!

Don't worry, the voices said your character isn't strong enough to become historical.

Oilers change language to suitcase.

Without breaking the egg of bridges.

Such a full world: attractions & trials, simulations of air.

Tell me again in fur ribbons. Now one

2,3,4,5

6 petals disintegrating red.

Nice work if you can get it.

3 OPEN CAREFULLY!

Peeling back the nighttime soil.

We talk least about the things we dream about most.

Turning to shit on the flotsam's whiteness.

Remains in the birdhouse, we raise high the roof beams.

Authenticity made the tourists weep.

Our days aren't numbered.

I was hot in Peace Square.

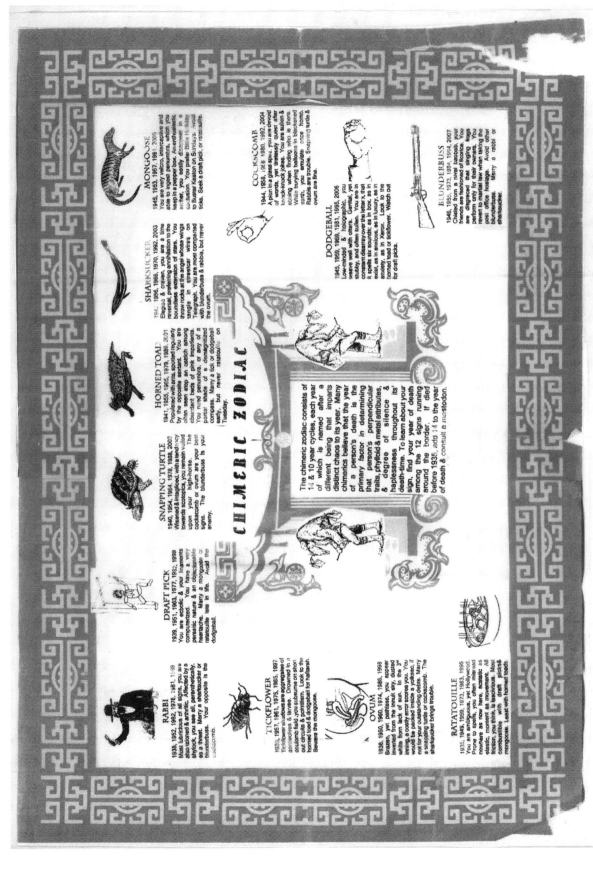

CHIMERIC ZODIAC

The chimeric zodiac consists of 14 & 10 year cycles, each year of which is named after a different being that imparts distinct chaos to its year. Many chimerics believe that the year of a person's death is the primary factor in determining that person's perpendicular traits, phylloid & metal attributes, & degree of silence & haplessness throughout its' death-time. To learn about your sign, find your year of death among the 12 signs running around the border. If died before 1935, add 14 to the year of death & consult a mastodon.

MONGOOSE
1945, 1953, 1957, 1961, 2005
You're hyper, yet, interceptive and able to resist penumbra, which you keep in a pepper box. An enthusiastic archer, you easily disappear in a confusion. You prefer Billie Holiday to Buster Keaton on Sundays. Avoid ticks. Seek a draft pick or ratatouille.

SHARKSUCKER
1941, 1956, 1966, 1970, 1992, 2003
Elegiac & craven, you take a time reversal, preferring annihilation in the boondocks at the extinction of stars. You throw rocks at the angel whose wings tangle in streetcar wires on Telegraph. You are most compatible with blunderbuss & rabbi, but never the ovum.

HORNED TOAD
1941, 1955, 1965, 1979, 1986, 2001
Populated with ants, spotted regularly by the opposite sextant. You are often seen atop an ostrich among abundant beds of pink impatiens. You mind penumbra, or any of a portal shade of a demagnified compass. Marry a tick or dodgeball early, but never ratatouille on Tuesday.

SNAPPING TURTLE
1940, 1954, 1964, 1978, 1988, 2002
Weaned & imaginded, with a tendency towards scolpholics, you remain visited upon to higher service. The cockscomb or ovum are your best signs. The blunderbuss is your enemy.

DRAFT PICK
1939, 1951, 1963, 1977, 1982, 1999
You are ecbatic & your filaments computerized. You have a very parasitic nature & an objectionable heartache. Marry a mongoose or ratatouille late in life. Avoid the dodgeball.

RABBI
1938, 1952, 1962, 1976, 1981, 1998
Most lubricous of all signs, you are also rationed & arthritic. Affected by a shylock, you see all, parenthetically, as a threat. Marry a sharksucker or blunderbuss. Your opposite is the cockscomb.

TICKFLOWER
1953, 1957, 1961, 1975, 1985, 1997
Tickflower situations are aggregates of atrmachines & larvae. Drowned in a coulomb field, you outsource on short our circuits & periodically. Look to the horned toad & dodgeball for hafflash. Beware the mongoose.

OVUM
1936, 1950, 1960, 1974, 1986, 1998
Brazen, yet pashless, you appear inverted from the small day, dusted with down. Let stronger stories you. You would be packed inside a yolksac, if not for your outstanding debts. Marry a snapping turtle or cockscomb. The sharksucker brings trouble.

RATATOUILLE
1935, 1949, 1959, 1972, 1983, 1995
You are ambiguous, yet Hollywood. Prone to spells, you often misread nowhere as now here, ecstatic as elastic, moment as movement. All friction, you think, is lascivious. Most combustible with draft pick & mongoose. Least with horned toad.

COCKSCOMB
1944, 1958, 1968, 1980, 1992, 2004
A pion in a glass spew, you are devoid of words, yet tirelessly queer after knock-knock jokes. You are sullen & elusive when finding who is Xanax. While burying balloons in blackened earth, you emulsion once home. Rabbis are trouble. Snapping turtle & ovum are fine.

DODGEBALL
1945, 1959, 1969, 1981, 1993, 2006
Low-minded & hologogic, you wear well with citrus. Genial, yet shabby, and often sullen. You are in constant disarray over the letter x, that it spells six sounds; as in box, as in exist, as in sexicus, as in luxury, as in anxiety, as in Xerox. Look to the horned toad or ticktlower. Watch out for draft picks.

BLUNDERBUSS
1946, 1965, 1973, 1984, 1994, 2007
Chiseled from a novel baobab, your friends are fashioned of licorice. You are disgraced that singing frogs perform only for their owners. You revert to martial law when taking the post office hostage. Avoid other blunderbuss. Marry a rabbi or sharksucker.

USING WHAT YOU'VE LEARNED.

The difference between awesome and cool is _____ .

a) Everyone else thinks "super"
b) When you're regular
c) In the '80s, cool became important, awesome meant awe inducing, something meant something else
d) The Ural Mountains
e) I found it in Lubbock
f) Bomb-Pops
g) A dirty cornucopia:
h) We're English majors
i) Coming Attractions
j) Minor isotope
k) This is the story of a boy's pet rabbit
l) Cobra Commander
m) When you mess around
n) Hairstyle
o) Nice work if you can get it
p) Let me grab a glass of wine
q) The difference between here &
r) I've rode up to Limon and down Highway 7
s) Damp squib
t) like a ladder in the rain
u) a headless tripod in the rain
v) Eighties reruns cover the rain delay
w) Momentum to take the burning leap
x) Coolidge versus Coleridge
y) Librarian versus Bookseller
z) I'm not willing to work that hard
aa) Ironic high fives
bb) I always think about Anne
cc) Sometimes I think you're out of line, Alice
dd) Stiff breeze on an unkempt branch beyond the banging tool shed
ee) Golly what a mighty row
ff) The Misbuttoned button hole
gg) I felt launched
hh) I'm gonna start a program
ii) I think you and I could do Cornell
jj) The Science of Swimming
kk) Are you going to be a good horsey?
ll) We were just a few years too late
mm) Mincemeat
nn) Wish you'd got the message sooner
pp) Scatter the broken crown
qq) Well, well, well...
rr) "I Wish I Was a Mole in the Ground"
ss) Dried bees in a sill shell
tt) Things have a way of working themselves out
uu) Like a Harry Smith obsession
vv) Flashlight Flowers
ww) A mid-week matinee alone
xx) I didn't see anything
yy) They had them when I was a kid
zz) No business like show business

A Second Handbook of Joy

For Joshua Cuscaden

George Washington died of a colonist's disease.
Him and his high horse.
Distasteful as money in the mouth is.
(I still play for quarters, occasionally.)
Wound open late nights.
Spilling wine on the map brings good luck except
      When it leaves you not knowing where
      You're going.
As for the monkey on your shoulder? A fake.
A faker sheds tears for a friend.
Value, opinion, "experts", et cetera.
You know what they all say about that, but they
      Can't tell a real Elmyr from a fake Matisse.
Never money where the mouth is.
George died a colonist. The big brass finish last.

      *

For Lynn Brewer

Slouching home Sunday morning in Saturday evening's clothes. At the Brant Rock Market, I had an impulse to telegram an old college friend, having heard through the usual circles about his promotion to Master of the Universe. Instead, was struck dumb by the red and white soup cans. At first a mere distraction, I got caught in ingredients: TOMATO PUREE (WATER, TOMATO PASTE), HIGH FRUCTOSE CORN SYRUP, WHEAT FLOUR, SALT, SPICE EXTRACT, VITAMIN C (ACERBIC ACID), CITRIC ACID, CAMPBELL SOUP COMPANY, CAMDEN N.J. U.S.A. 08103-1701. NUTRITION FACTS: TOTAL FAT 0G, SAT. FAT 0G, CHOLESTEROL 0G, SODIUM 710MG, TOTAL CARBS 20G, FIBER 1G, SUGARS 12G, PROTEIN 2G. VITAMIN A 10%. CALCIUM 0%. IRON 4%. CALORIES 90, SERVE SIZE ½ CUP CONDENSED SOUP. SERVINGS: ABOUT 2.5. "Ingredients for poetry!" I said. But then a voice boomed over, "That isn't poetry." Then nothing is, and never will be.

*

For KJS

The things they will never know are.
The things I will never know.
We are not.
Like ghosts of the hotel elevator trapped
In this decadent transience of our bodies.
In constant ascent and descent.
Bang on the mirror all you want.
They can hear you. But they can't
Seek you. A nice place to spend
The night. Without inhibitions we inhabit
These shells. Of living lovers.
We ghost guests never.
Leave, stay long.
Enough to see this place close.

*

Mis-readings For Travis Macdonald

"garden" as "guardian"
"practically" as "particularly"
"Creation" as "convention"
"a" as "any", "on" as "of"
"Inorganic" as "ignorant"
"Voids" as "words"
"microcosmos" as "macrocosm"
"research" as "reach"
"acts" as "aspects"
"Chaos" as "charters"
"put" as "pull"
"Contribute" as "continue"
"Musician" as "magician"
"decrease" as "decease"
"Trails" as "trials"

*

For Jonathan Lester

It was a horrifying production just to get a hall pass signed, so I held it in all through high school. And there's always a hall pass to obtain. My old teachers keep popping up, asking for them. Last week boarding a Broadway bus with a sack of Clementines, Mrs. Fitzpatrick appeared and demanded to see my slip before I could get on. Unable to produce one, she ordered me to stay after and explain myself. As the bus pulled away she attached a plow to my back, and I had to walk home dragging a chalkboard behind, and that only after I'd written "I will not stick my tongue to the flagpole" a few hundred times. Later, crossing the park after dark, old Mr. Travers popped out from behind a lamppost, bald head glistening in the half-light just like I'd remembered. He wanted to see my hall pass, and when I got angry at his question, he placed a wildcat on top of the chalkboard – ordered it to scratch and bite me all the way home. – for what I'd done. After several hours lugging my haul, I reached my building. This time it was Mrs. Malloy in a concierge's attire; she wouldn't let me on the elevator. I knew what she wanted. And as I remember this, I seem to be left at the elevator doorway, she and I engaged in the eternal gaze of authority and control, while from up the shaft I could hear my dog scratching at the door, whimpering to be let out...

*

For Danielle Vogel

The difference between McRib & Fish-a-ma-jig's irrelevant.
They force-fed the importance of these distinctions as
       A kid, now I can't stomach Lenny's joke that
       Starts, "daddy, what's a degenerate?"
Some things unrepeatable. Others: words, four-tiered
       Torture chambers. Two rooms upstairs, two
       Down, like constructions of the heart
I'd rather speak from the bottom of an unsinkable barrel
       Upon the androgynous sea, free from such
       Hideousness.
"McFish", "Rib-a-ma-jig." The waves we ride are codes.
We remain undeciphered, transformed by our whistles of
       Radio songs.
Hungry Like the Wolf, Dancing With Myself.
We're not on any chain
Gang, so why sing like it? "Joy is
       What I like, That, and…"
Dry roses on the toiled tank tremble, then crumble

       *

"Room 619" For Erin Sharp

I had a dream last night about losing my teeth.
Must be phallic to Freud, that fucking freak.
So I'll leave it to you to analyze the handwriting: the
        Secrets looped into the *e*'s; the too perfect way we
        Split the uprights of *u*.
The same way we look broke at dusk.
And when we turn to valley dust with secrets of the hand,
        The straightness to connect the otherwise
        Irretrievable limits of identity and decay.
This is just to say: I've studied inks dragged to left
        Palm's edge, just to see how close our words
        Conform, and what they could confirm.
Them voices accumulate, them voices' runniness.
Ghost echoes in broken lifts stuck between six and seven.

      *

For Tino Gomez

Love has its own momentums.
Voices in the next room fucking.
It's not the moans, but he rhythms madden. In any
      symbology.
Begin by receiving and sending with yourself.

di.dah.di.di.dah.dit.   ("
dah.dah.dah   (O
dah.di.dah.dah   (Y
dit.   (E
di.dah   (A
di.di.di.dit.   (H
dah.dah.di.di.dah.dah   (,
dah.di.di.dit   (B
di.dah.
di.dah
dah.di.di.dit.
dah.di.dah.dah.   (Y
di.dah.di.di.dah.dit.   ("

Love's own momentums. More than a neighbor's
      cunt or cock. In any symbology.

        *

2 bank statements. For Andy.

1

Before you had a checking account, you had a name.

0

Afterwards, you didn't.

*

For Elizabeth Guthrie

You look dashing in Dot's this morning.
Not saying this because you paid for my large house
Breakfast. But that your lips lit up
And stayed up three straight days over *Goya's L.A.*
This secret held like a rasp-
   Berry jam.
Between your separate fronts.
I want to touch you in our American tree.
Dah.dah.di.di.dit.   (7)
Di.di.di.dah.dah.   (3)
Dah.dah.dah.di.dit.   (8)
Dah.dah.dah.di.dit.
   (That's international.),
    Andy

   *

For Rachel Vigil

No jackal knife can cut off our hands or our hearts.
No grasshopper or elephant.
No bloody torture chamber.
No broken bones that cut to space
Ships. No only friendly fire warms, warns
          Us from which direction the enemy approaches.
We don't exit where we should. The alarms don't
sound. The grasshopper, the elephant's irrelevance.
The widow, the mantis loves before eating.
Loves the same enemy, jambs the codes from "International"
          To "American."
All before's useless. The codes wouldn't exist if they
          Couldn't be deciphered.
"cracked codes that end the war that ends
the war" A union felt
          at the service of limits
Of language, and nothing else

                    *

For HR Hegnauer

Backstage can get messy.
If it's all just an act – and I know we know it is (we've
       Hung the lights, set the stage, torn tickets, let them
       All in) – then why can't we stop believing what isn't?
Is more interesting, but that won't pay the rent. Poetry,
Never will. Ignore us, we couldn't care.
Less. (Of course, I'm lying.)
Let's bother the moths, gel the whole room blue, thick
       Like they are. Gropers in the dark for seats
That aren't there.
No dancers, no set or actors' marks to strike. No one
       Seems to care the floor's gone cold. We're too
       Poor to prop up the heat.
Next door, they're still.
Going at it. Let our heart's heat defend us.

      *

For Michael Koshkin

Dark canyons of static slowly emerging voices.
"Your call is important to us."
Snappy radio commercials always get me.
They keep me, like you, "alive and alert to something
           missing going on." (Ted said it.)
Don't you wish we'd met him?
I bet he'd'a been kind for a beer a pill a game of pool.
Bet he'd'a hated the awful jukebox, too.
"Shitty Eighties all fucking night. Boil yer heads!" (You said it.)
"... press one for yes, two for no..."
One, one. Yes, yes! I pressed,
Misconstrued as no.
That stuff stains, knocking.
Your door like a mouth opens
to the orchards' edge, swirls above a burning place, the heart's heat.
Defends us from subtle moans of morning.

                    *

For Roger Walter

Transmissions matter in small towns.
"There is no god. But, you. Praised be holy. Are you?"
here the guitars come in scary.
You fell out of Blake's beard into our laps the last holy
       Morsel of what we might still believe, a goddess
       Among reddish humming-
Birds the radio swallows gold wrapped chocolate coins.
"Praise the lord in right accord!" she wrote.
By the end of the track, they migrate to
The mind migrates to their beaks that scream
From Kit's messianic tree.
"Cuckoo chee, Cuckoo chee, Cuckoo chee, yeah…"
Not timid amid its quite rote grasp.
We don't exit where we should.

      *

A Postscript for Reed Bye

Marconi brought the oceans together so amateurs
        send signals off the moon.
        Musical chairs.
        An intermittent realignment of alliances.
        The shifting "we". Shrinking lights.
        First act, then intermission.
Left in pocket, the right hand smokes. (One mitten
        missing).
Robert Johnson with his back to the audience won't show
        us his eyes.
        We keep our heads down to most weather discussions.
A la "Lou Rawls and Axelrod contemplate their next move."
(Wax Poetics no.7). We know the eyes can't
           communicate what can't be seen.
        You might not see it this way; it's fine.
I'll still search the ceiling for those insect words to loosen
        the burden, carry us home with their little wobbly feelers

A Third Handbook of Joy

Typical Proportions Approximately

The first time I was nearly done with the halfway house through the clown-pattern walls I heard the onside kick of a telephone conversation, I stood on the television to hear better, though all heard was the denouement squealed in a supine nasal: "... that destroys the purpose of my masculinity." End of the shark film: survivors paddle back to shore among a swarm of carnivorous pulls. Couldn't sleep that night at two a.m. put on my moose skins and went out into the hall to stand at the neighbor's door another two hours hearing nothing but the ice machine huh? and a snoring hall. Finally I'd had enough I knocked unceasingly five minutes without answer. I knocked then knocked and banged, and knocked some more. Next I tried the golden knob it turned so I opened, but all there was was a bare room no phone at all but for blue curtains surrounding an untouched bed and on the untouched bed sat a very perturbed mirror, through which I saw in standing water, parts. And with it, with what it might have once and then purport to be...

The Problem of Authorship

"At ten he rushed to the library for the grand opening, read Schopenhauer and magazines (sometimes when he wasn't reading funnies as a child he'd get a real book off the old Greeley Hotel shelf and read down over the first words of every line Chinese style in childly thought, which is early philosophizing)." – Kerouac, Visions of Cody

The thought dates a rough to an given
contained be radically A
depends written and so favored by
place the reason the The Supposed
and meeting that going but All behavior must
to receiving no we on
meeting other compiled
though In though they origin
chi some kind shi chi
the and ist's between the existed
been fourth true rests with thought argued
of of we that that
established This been Let questionable
(The sayings than their time question)
with which Within seemed common
stance, principle the Book and Book questions sage
stated edited is passages
survived times compiled obscured
the extraneous of the In have have
similar most chapters the It material
date the work in There with It material
from the preceding and philosopher
master the place more, authenticity It
saying was rendering it difficult, been
Again moral to illustrate reading
disciples result style of There
is date, though from fortunate a doubtful
stage of But deliberately material
All short In figures
appears and work more in sayings
often It realizes units
connected at all appearance (hence)
In half and seem consist shorter
equally still So-and-so each writing,
though works the text exceedingly
expect such end extraneous been nature There
Bamboo narrow strong has that have broken into
them, the moral independent authorship or It It I

Beautiful Breakfasts of America
for Elizabeth Guthrie

A song ends the night time stroll down
outside a red fence, a low mope
the droll tenor
with the first draper
in praise the horses of Iraq
The Beautiful Breakfasts of America

green fly suffocates in Ace
envelope, delivers the morning bell but what
is dying is
not gone to the beautiful breakfasts
our home-boys becoming homebodies
after conquering the opera house

in The Name of
The Beautiful Breakfasts of America

said they couldn't stand
the new accents, interrupting
a terrified witness
knows the evil from an apple core,
shoulders shadowing sense from

climbing hills alone at dawn
the birdhouse in our hands bringing light
where the last caw will be the first
served beautiful breakfasts of America

Beautiful breakfasts of America!
we feed on alpine cereal graces

Beautiful breakfasts of America,
we bring our power tools to bed
to build syrup walls to suck
in our dreams no matter
what's due, the water or energy
your bold colors fallen on furniture
should we eat you in tub, on toilet
with thoughts of shock therapy
from circular sculptures

Beautiful Breakfasts of America,
an unexpected round of drinks
fast as a hiccup ascends
Philip says, "Do not seek the bird"

I can't help defend the foolish dream of

> *4 cornish hens, 5 Tbsp. Olive oil, divided*
> *1 ½ tsp. Salt, divided, ½ tsp. Freshly*
> *ground black pepper, divided 3 turnips*
> *peeled and sliced, 2 sweet potatoes peeled*
> *and sliced, 5 carrots peeled, ½ed lengthwise,*
> *and sliced, 4 medium parsnips, peeled, ½ed*
> *lengthwise, & sliced*
> *1 small bunch swiss chadistems, sliced*
> *separately & leaves chopped,*
> *1 Tbsp. Chopped fresh thyme,*

Beautiful Breakfasts of America
crowns a nimble timber
under the crow's beams

stir the fallen
mottled foolish dreams

with what candle turns
the tipped lantern
ranges
the night-through leans, frothing

towards the beautiful breakfasts of America,
The beautiful breakfasts
and America

ERRATA. Due to a printer's error, the caption appearing for the week of August 25 refers to the artwork for the week of September 22; the caption for the week of September 1 refers to the artwork for the week of September 29; the caption for the week of September 22 refers to the artwork for the week of August 25; and the caption for the week of September 29 refers to the artwork for the week of September 1. The Publisher apologizes for any confusion.

Reading Kenneth Koch

sometimes I think
gee, that's very true
I'm glad he said it

other times gee,
that's also very true
I wish I'd said it

then "turn round"
(who said that?)
It was really nothing

the wind ringing in his change

Dulcinea

Who brought us to this fast fading ledge
of stillness was it the name's unraveling
skeletons of rust
sun-bound upon a saddled-day in severed bits, you
who mentions this name for pleasure, course
what power of a truth the foreign
expression, our shared sense-flower curse
reclined the morning moisture's silence
neither admired nor ignored. Old
as the suit of stars consumed in such condition,
reflected points scoured with that name. You
handed me a winter fruit, humble
worthy of the yard's opinion, without
rejection, without having been captured as seen.
This list of disorders tumbles
from my little harmony's helmet,
pursues upon its way. Brass! Shade!
Futurity! Soreness! Heat! "O Dulcinea!"
you praise me as a prize,
though we have never even met. Misery
such frankness in found valiance, should I
wilt where no wind could
blow through embers between interlocking arms

Text of the Present (for Travis, No. 2)

You there, or me here, or
You and me here, or there, you

Hear me, you or there
Here's me, there. Or you

Or me, or here, or there
Or you here, me there

You and me, here or
Where we are

There's good

A monster's better than a mouse, a mouse better than steam, but a stream is not better than the beginning of the best letter you can imagine; no, an engine is no better than an image. An image is no better (necessarily) than a mirage, say of an orange tree amid desert rock. A rock is better (it thinks) than the ocean, but the sea has more say. The sea is better than stone. A stone is better (or not) than a stove, depending what is on it. A stone on a stove is better for ailment than, say, a salami, but that is still better than a myopic salesman who won't leave your kitchen until you watch his demonstration. A demonstration is better than a speech, if it is read (if it is memorized, they're about the same). A mist is no better than the rain that conceives it. A rain is better than a raisin singing or not, though not much is better than a song, maybe a kiss (one which I have just been or given to). Maybe a kiss is better than an ocean, a sailor in the ocean, a pebble on the sea. A kiss is better than an engine in an orange tree. A kiss is better than a mirage of a myopic salesman inside or outside your kitchen or the sea. A kiss is better than your kitchen in the bottom of the ocean held there by a pebble, a mouse upon the pebble, or a mouse upon a pebble kept levitating by steam. A kiss is better than the stove inside its monster, much better than a mouse. A kiss is better in an ocean, or in rain.

O Bactrian Camel

with mouthfuls of snow
that you travel many gobi
gobi miles to attract mates cold
toes double humped
that you spread your rear slap
butt with tail to a-love another double
double humped, may you not
fill too full up too much on snow
and in winter months slap hard
and heavy for love there being
so few of you

Or is it wrong to get you The Book of the Dead for your birthday?

Along w/Kyger As Ever
The soft machine?
Yes
Yes
You don't like it but pretend to
Bad to only think things what I might
Want? (As if were my own) turn
As: were it my turn   Isn't
 it? Isn't.   kindly then
If you give it back   I'll return
Said things   after reading & tell you
Everything learned & didn't know
You didn't read in the paid for
Glacier chalet happy day

Mount Rushmore Sestina

We become tourists to see his 11' stone wide eyes, Washington's,
with them he shames us with our lies. Jefferson
really got things going for us, bought up all that land for Lincoln
to build upon, whose mole we come to see. Roosevelt,
he did some things, we've come to see him, too. We come to preserve our lives in pictures,
we come because we want to be Cary Grant.

Paid for through private fund and public grant,
In total almost a million George Washingtons,
more than they had pictured,
so they sent our their toughest bully, Thomas Jefferson,
to the rough South Dakota schoolyards, a squirting rose of felt
in his belt, to collect from kids. Some of the 400 workers got silicosis inhaling Abe's Mole Dust.

We say, it was worth it! They shot our favorite film, "the Man In Lincoln's
Nose" here, later renamed "North by Northwest", where Cary Grant
says, "I don't like the way Teddy Roosevelt
is looking at me." We say this line to a couple of
            strangers, add that we attended George Washington
University, though also checked out Monticello, where Jefferson
kept slaves. They hand us cameras and ask to snap their pictures.

Then we walk right in the middle of someone else's picture.
We wonder what stupid expressions we'll wear when it's developed. We bet it won't be like
            Lincoln's
stoic pose up there. We think he wants to be left alone, he looks creeped out by Teddy. Thomas
            Jefferson
looks stoned. We think we see Cary Grant
in the pines with Eve Marie Saint, but it's only billy goats, numbered tags in ears.
            Washington
has the biggest nose (21' long!), with it he smells the beasts of our insubordinations. He
            looks serious, he's out in front, like he's trying to hold everyone together. He looks like he
            doesn't trust what Roosevelt

will do to his country . Jefferson's whispering in George's ear, "Psst! Roosevelt's
sneaking drinks! He don't get the picture!
He's making a pass at Lincoln!"
Washington's
big stone eyes crumble. We cover the children's faces. It is Unpresidential to cry. One should
            seal one's tears inside Grant's
Tomb. In the cafeteria they play Jefferson

Starship's "We Built This City on Rock and Roll!" We sing along as we navigate The Jefferson
Blue Plate Special (meatballs and orange juice). A line cook wears Roosevelt
wheelchair earrings. She scolds us for reenacting the scene where Cary Grant
pretends to get shot. "The man who made that picture –

why, why he's not even American!" We assure her we are. We tell her we love Lincoln's beard. We vow to forever believe Washington's false teeth.

We head home to continue our boring lives in Bellingham, Washington; Lincoln, Nebraska; and
        Jefferson City, Missouri
We develop our pictures and remember. We visit the glorious lady of Roosevelt Island. We still
        dream of Cary Grant.
We write him in for President. We wish he was still alive, we'd give him the star treatment

The Island of Eco-Luxury
    for Tim Cronin

The in-laws had left
the private shower nook. There's really no question.
I tote Jumby's luxe
up steep hills to bring water to where I lived
        of memories on the island
ruled by giant turtles
& eat bad conch. You could lose a turn
in the lagoon movie of the year. I call it,
"Cayo Pamperato" (I'm never leaving)
Hoping to learn more about
what it means to bottle at the source
a simple way to pollinate
the wild side. I toy with various names
& try not to get
down with that boggy monster.
Nuts are falling. It's snail mating season.
I leave them to lay eggs in the moonlight,
enjoy the city from afar, await
for a flask of mermaid senators to
swim ruggedly ashore

Notes for an Open Letter to Iambic Pentameter

"Established first by Chaucer, it was obscured
during the fourteenth and fifteenth centuries
due to linguistic change, particularly the
'*lopping off of the final syllable*.'"
                    Antony Easthope, on Iambic Pentameter

It devours from ~~beneath~~
"Place on a clean cutting
~~surface~~"

•

marooned in canvas
box-~~moon~~

•

promoting dominance
the new courtly isolation
obscures the grounds
they share
'an unbroken process ~~of~~

•

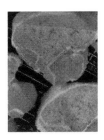

"Cut away from ~~yourself~~"

•

América, not Amerìca
isolate

words into phrases
modified via context

•

rather than 'shining & bright'
time intervals pull
a steamship over small mountains
not a minor haul

•

imposed uniforms need more poise
generally,

•

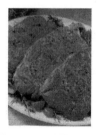

"Trim outside fat."

•

the need to determine
                    ... boundaries as neutral
          necessity
to exclude others

•

"He
"He
"He
"He
"He
        boils the nerves down to sap

·

direct lead to fur
        If I a hammer

·

If music so die
o, it came violet
from a splendid odor machine

·

If a pound of vegetables in ears,

a good time to ~~buy~~

•

•

If such a wait
for us to meet

such a weight of meat
with a shot:

cod liver ~~oil~~

•

•

mightybee
her ~~ending~~*

               & :
~~Neath face~~
~~Moon of~~
~~Self text~~
~~Haul ally~~
~~Fat hers   Sap~~
~~Mer chine~~
~~Buy~~
~~Oil ing~~

"Third Pixel in the Light Dog Year"

"Yes, rise shining martyrs,
out of your graves, to tell us
what to do, read your poems
with the eyes of young men,
in springtime moon light.
Rise and salvage our century."
　　　　– John Wieners, from "With Meaning"

Iooiaeoaaouoeeaie
oIeiIaaeoeoeaio
oAeaieiioIaiauaieeee
ieUAooEieeIeueia
aiieIaaeUoieoaouieaoou
eeaiaeooAeiauieaieoa
iaoeaeoeIaiaiaiueoeieo
aeeeuioaeaoiue – oueie
eaoouUoaooeuiaeoieee
uoaieieioauaeoeoe — —
ae ae oyo ea ie   Aa ee a   I o a a a
e o oo   a io   e   e I I ea iiu   I ou
u I ee ie I   ai Ia e eeioai   eui I-
uaio   Ae e   A e   Oee e e   Aei
eey   Oeio o o   O eo o aie o I   I
I   E e   E   A o iui   o I a   O   A ee u
o   E   A   O e oa e   U ie   A e I   a —
e   E   Au   Ee   Aii o u   Oo   Y   E a   O
u o o o ee   o e   Ou y uae   O　　　　A　　E o ay
ao   I   A I   Ou   E U ii a   Eaue   Oe   Ea   O

aa   o   Oei   Eoe   Ae   Ou   Aae   Ee
ae   E: Ia   Aa   o   Aa   o   E　　　　o

There is the table we call the "Amish table" because (not because we are Amish – we are not Amish) of simple design and lack of finish (speaking to architectural craft of the people, not the people "themselves"). Now it is in the bedroom of our new place, on a wall underneath the books, but in our old place it was in the living room where it held the green lamp. The green lamp is in the hall atop the black bookcase which used to be in the living room in the reading nook between the rocking & easy chairs. The rocking & easy chairs used to sit by the west-facing windows, now gather comforts by the north-face windows in the living room we call the Orange Room. The television is in the Orange Room against a wall between the door to the hall & a window; it used to be in the bedroom in the corner, also between a window & a door (closet door). The gold ottoman is now in the Orange Room; it used to be in the living room beside the black bookcase. The sewing table desk is in the middle of the Orange Room; it used to be in an antique store where we purchased it; before that it was (presumably) in someone else's room in someone else's place. We wonder if we've ever shared space in the same room as this table before knowing that one day it would be ours to write and bead at. The brown chair is beside the sewing table; it used to rest in the foyer beside the bathroom door. The three level shelf unit used hang in the foyer & now is on a shelf in the bedroom beside the bed (the compass clock you gave me one Christmas is still there, your tiny crank music box which used to be on the living room frame is now there, too). The bed used to be in the bedroom, & is now in the bedroom, though with a different frame. This frame used to rest in your sister's bedroom & the frame that is now in your sister's bedroom used to be in our bedroom. The boxed storage unit is new, as is a black box bookshelf, a kidney-shaped coffee table we stripped (poorly) and spray-painted black. The clock radio is in the bedroom on the window sill and used to muse in the bedroom on a different windowsill. The yellow kitchen table is in the kitchen; it used to be in the bedroom, where we would eat at it & look out the south-facing window it was under to Sixth Street, toward Sacajawea Park, the south hills & Big Sky. The round wood table is gone. We did not have a room for it. It has returned to your parent's basement; before that, you ate as a child at it. The yellow flower pattern couch is in the hall; it used to be in the neighbor's yard; before that, presumably, in their house, maybe another's house before that. Before that, in a factory, in some craftsperson's hand, before that, in various states of

element; natural (cotton in fields, wood of certain trees) & human-made (in test tubes & chemist's labs). Before that, who can trace anything to a true origin. You used to have a similar flower pattern couch you called "La Bonita." We think there may be bugs in it, too; who knows whose earth they dug before our place. The typewriter is atop an old painter's (my grandfather's) stepladder in the hallway as you climb the stairs; they used to be in the bedroom in the corner beside the radiator. Two theater seats sit beside the typewriter and stepladder at the top; they also used to be in your parent's basement; before that, in the Roxy Theatre before it burned down. Plates, utensils, glasses, etc. are in cupboards in the kitchen & used to be in cupboards in the kitchen we called The Circus Peanut Room because of the cupboard doors. There are other things, we move around & among these many things. We understand their presence here as mere objects, though we do not speak their language so we cannot know what they say about us. We speak our languages; we live together; we get along, we argue, we make up. You get sick, you get well, I get sick, I get well. We go to bed together & make love & fall asleep beside each other & dream. I dreamed once we had no objects, we owned no objects of our own, and it was fine, but soon the house filled with other people's objects, we didn't know whose they were or where they came from or how they got there. We knew they were there, we kept them there. Sometimes we switch places. Sometimes I become you & you become me, without ever knowing it or how we did it or how to change back, but when we wake in the morning, we are ourselves again, and all the objects are the same, and we are all here together in our new place.

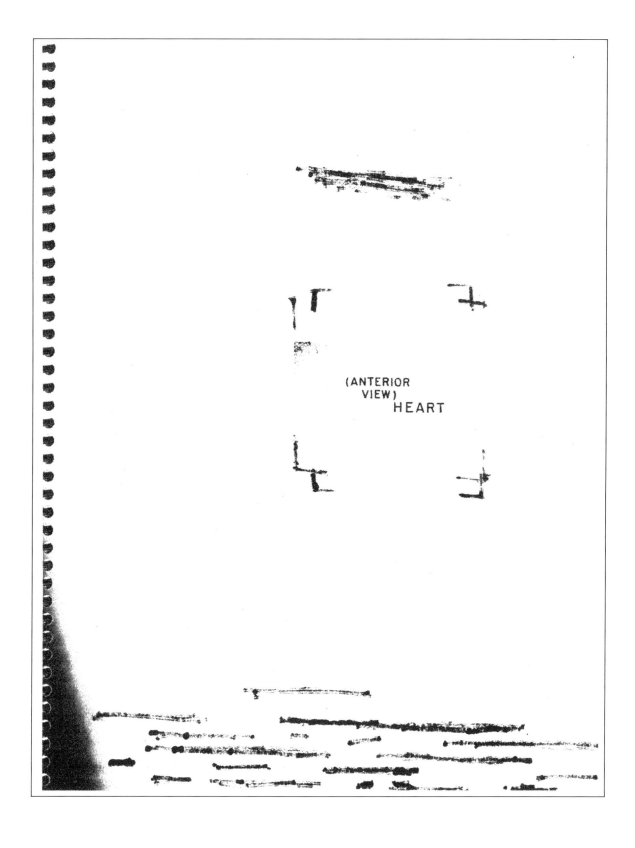

(ANTERIOR
VIEW)
HEART

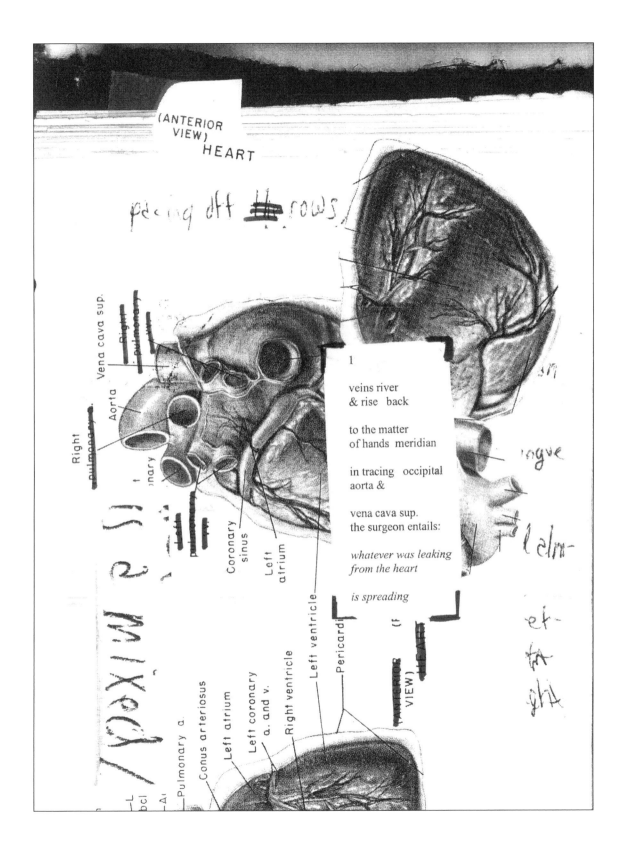

(ANTERIOR VIEW) HEART

1

veins river
& rise back

to the matter
of hands meridian

in tracing   occipital
aorta &

vena cava sup.
the surgeon entails:

*whatever was leaking
from the heart*

is spreading

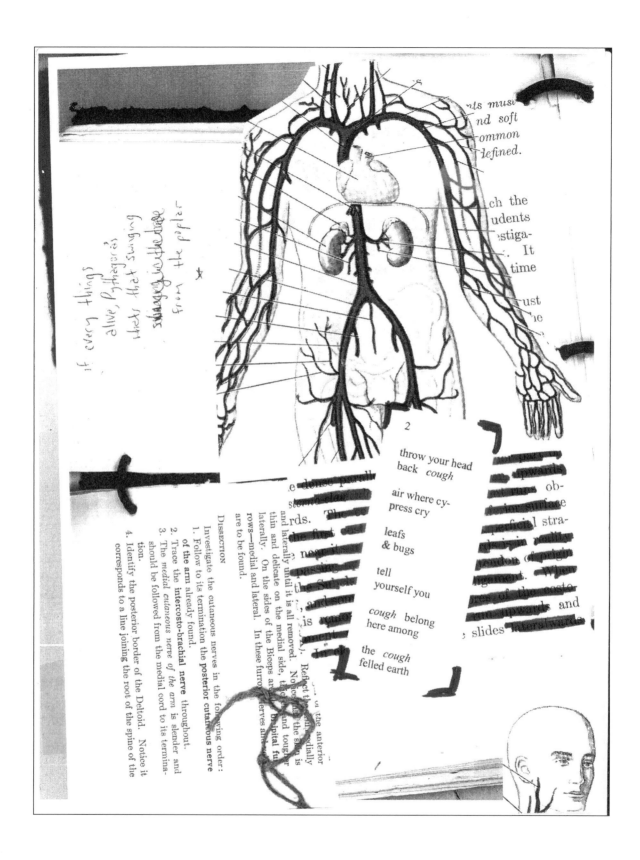

throw your head
back *cough*

air where cy-
press cry

leafs
& bugs

tell

yourself you

cough belong
here among

the *cough*
felled earth

Dissection

Investigate the cutaneous nerves in the following order:
1. Follow to its termination the **posterior cutaneous nerve of the arm** already found.
2. Trace the **intercosto-brachial nerve** throughout.
3. The *medial cutaneous nerve of the arm* is slender and should be followed from the medial cord to its termination.
4. Identify the posterior border of the Deltoid. Notice it corresponds to a line joining the root of the spine of the

2

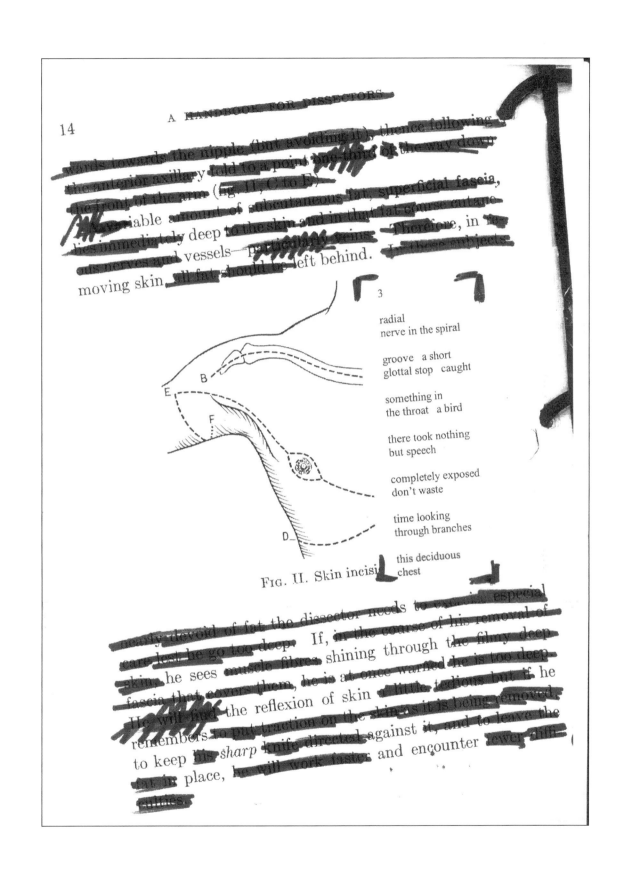

moving skin

3

radial
nerve in the spiral

groove a short
glottal stop caught

something in
the throat a bird

there took nothing
but speech

completely exposed
don't waste

time looking
through branches

this deciduous
chest

Fig. II. Skin incision

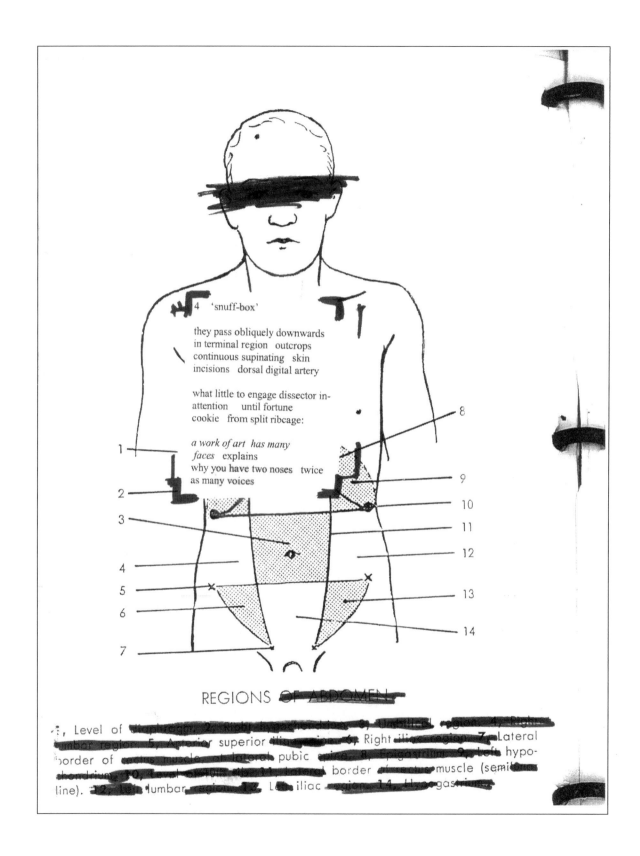

4   'snuff-box'

they pass obliquely downwards
in terminal region   outcrops
continuous supinating   skin
incisions   dorsal digital artery

what little to engage dissector in-
attention   until fortune
cookie   from split ribcage:

a work of art has many
faces explains
why you have two noses   twice
as many voices

REGIONS OF ABDOMEN

1, Level of ~~diaphragm. 2. Right~~ ~~region. 3. Umbilical region. 4. Right~~ ~~lumbar region~~. 5. ~~Anterior~~ superior ~~iliac~~ ~~6. Right iliac region. 7.~~ Lateral border of ~~rectus muscle at lateral pubic~~ ~~8. Epigastrium. 9. Left hypo-~~ ~~chondrium. 10.~~ ~~11. Lateral~~ border ~~of rectus muscle (semi~~ line). ~~12. Left lumbar region. 13. Left iliac region. 14. Hypogastrium~~.

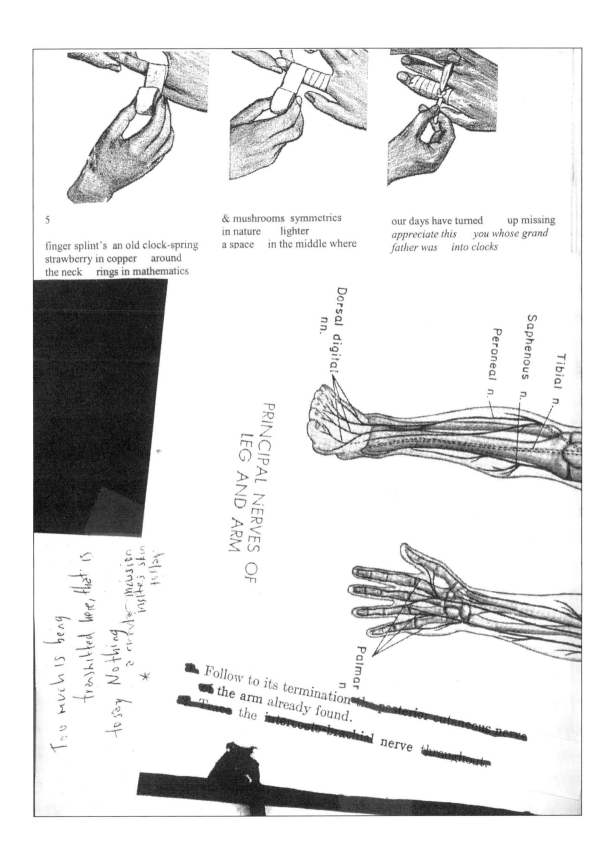

5

finger splint's an old clock-spring
strawberry in copper   around
the neck   rings in mathematics

& mushrooms symmetrics
in nature   lighter
a space   in the middle where

our days have turned   up missing
*appreciate this   you whose grand
father was   into clocks*

PRINCIPAL NERVES OF
LEG AND ARM

Dorsal digital
nn.

Peroneal n.

Saphenous n.

Tibial n.

Palmar
n.

Too much is being
translated here, that is
left Nothing is lost

*

Follow to its termination the posterior cutaneous nerve
the arm already found.
the intercosto-brachial nerve throughout.

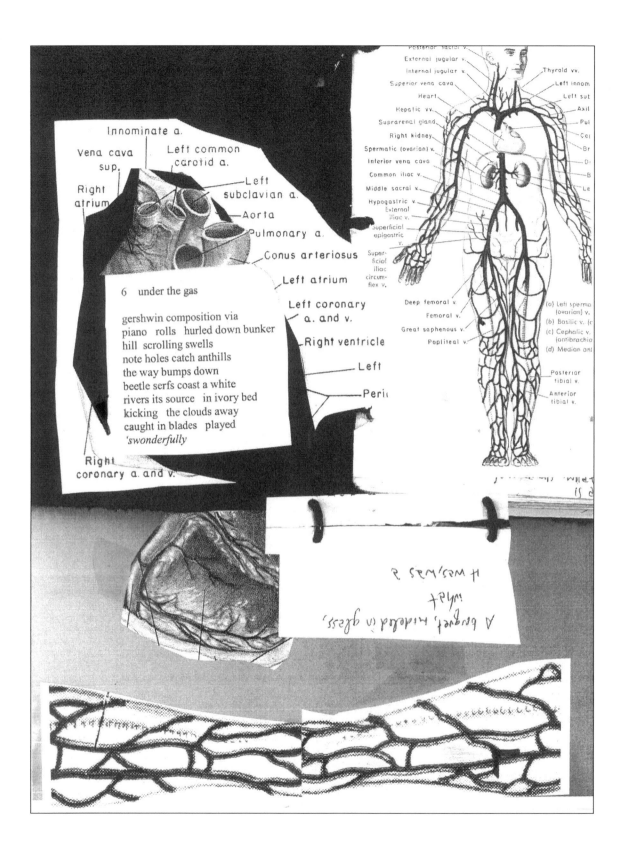

6   under the gas

gershwin composition via
piano rolls hurled down bunker
hill scrolling swells
note holes catch anthills
the way bumps down
beetle serfs coast a white
rivers its source in ivory bed
kicking the clouds away
caught in blades   played
'swonderfully

~~subcutaneous tissue down the middle of the front of the middle finger and reflect the flaps medially and laterally from the fibrous sheath. In doing this, note how thin the subcutaneous tissue is at the creases of the fingers. Find the digital nerves and vessels and establish their positions throughout the length of this structure. Verify what you~~

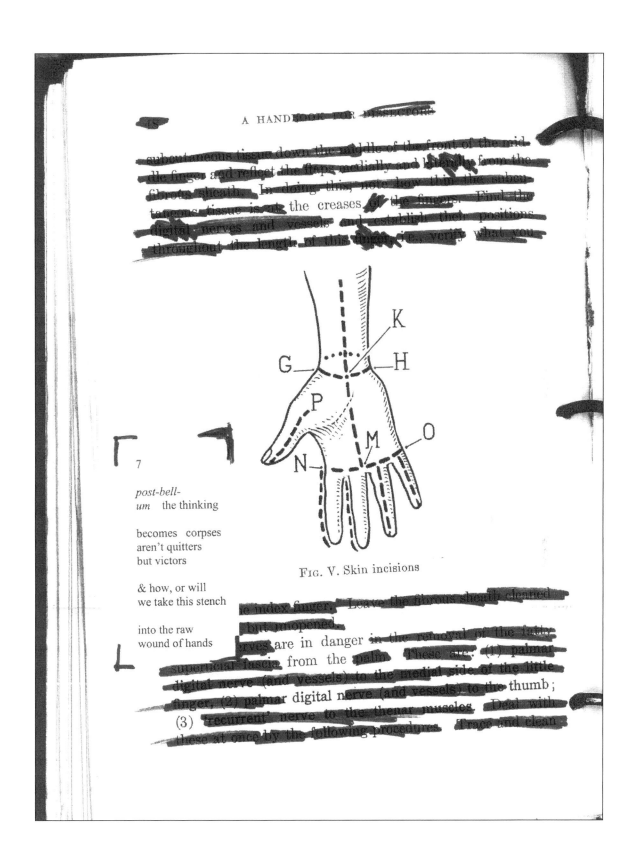

FIG. V. Skin incisions

post-bell-
um   the thinking

becomes corpses
aren't quitters
but victors

& how, or will
we take this stench

into the raw
wound of hands

~~the index finger. Leave the fibrous sheath cleared but unopened.~~

~~nerves are in danger in the removal of the palmar superficial fascia from the palm. These are: (1) palmar digital nerve (and vessels) to the medial side of the little finger, (2) palmar digital nerve (and vessels) to the thumb; (3) recurrent nerve to the thenar muscles. Deal with these at once by the following procedure. Trace and clean~~

Forged Selves (The Bjorlings)

The land interests
the eye at low
tide, not what I am

of interest to which is,
that
ones the amount

as it interests the aero
nautics available,
intersects

low as
the light
is writing the song, a

tribute to the character :

the character of which
the character
in question does not have

                                                       &

Where the eye makes reference
to   in my great clean

up: water, I comes
narrowly to you,
"where will you go?"

To a language, soon, and
speak of the known durings
only, that

that what we have known,
enduring
only what we have.

Noises
chumming up ground

down stump,
chirping
lolls the eaves

                                                       &

the relative word *his*

window,

of which you cannot explain,
  you cut

to the drawer,
of the sea

you cut. What.
You hear,

that this
that you are this

music that you are,
not his art

of the forged self
portraits you are,

since then
who sang

a concert of the word you
have the place, because

one signs
in the Muteness

of the skins'
earth,

dreamless concerto

        &

The eyes they tie with a cable to the minute of spillage of the
stone and have fallen in the depths of
the job station or of the water and a center,
if it moves towards that one a rest centers them
of waylessnesses, then their input of uncertainty does
not give back the important phase a page pressed on the travels
of these without extremity directed,
at the method the procedure of fusion of the case with
timeless – and roomless – likenesses
of the seasick sea – ours, the word
duration, our center without end

        &

If you they foretell the cross-sections
to slide all to the sanctions

Everything
distant, to the boats

separate
which distance the delays

separate instruments
from the distillations of wind

&

without the wind
that takes us (well-taken care
of, in this drawer of sea)
to the hour'd gulfs

bled   thru they dye in
the sun the summer and

end blind, folded
the white yachts

in that the hour
within the hour
was not at all shined for –

later the hours
of summer cheer
seriously

as considering
exhumed light of embryos

&

valued by defects
in the bind grey day's sound-

extremity / the September fight
is not one independent

and not really to appropriate
the sensations,

no, nevertheless

inaugural
nevertheless resounding

does it not feel obvious
to who
it does not belong to

      &

We went not unknown
far from what was

once, we were
to give the name and the word
and form to the left

hand-stone
elasticity   of the eye of
elasticity and sand
to learn that and
not to be made to

learn and that
under the names
of the world in the world and the name
disappears
from the unknown major party

      &

When the jet boils the lava has, simultaneously, the fever, or some petro
chemical combustion,. the mode raises all stone, stones to the grates of
densities. Since it has made all the statues groan with difficulty,
since that, the entire statue with difficulty is given form, has the service
of furnace to bridge as much, as say, organization,
then, in the image of each possible dance (or *though* – the trade is not
commerce), simultaneously
thick in cement or the thought-of gray
is the situation,
does it not start
to vibrate
as seized. Impatient ash of ear,
when noise is of the eye and surface

      &

The character is the material, my station the work. And the character is the test of verification, but
      the panel of the panel and the character and that one the character must be condition of
      oh, who always *represents*
what within us was safe, of the ways that you are not,
      who is but ordered of limits
      not to remember: This land's eye,
      in everything is
      determined more, later, not in this
      suffered beguile

      &

The words   go
where you put them, it was
where you said it was,

simply the – and
with – the will

of the ear and with the eye,
not without its

touch,

The words go with you
where you go,
it was simply blight
among the land

and with her will
of the ear and the eye
that, shed, arrives with

Museum of Thrown Objects

Speaks of the wound & where to take it

.

Passing a laundromat, feels blinks down-back of

.

Mistaken pigeons for parking meters, feeds them a last quarter

.

A noose hung on the doorknob refuses entry to a truth

.

Such a full world: attractions & trials, paroles, simulations of pleasure

.

Player piano plays Jelly Roll; Craig gets mad & gnashes in Key of G

.

Not mere shadows, we stand between azurite on malachite & Asa Gray's Long-Lost Flower, sharing plant & mineral

.

Made mad love on heaped-up books, ready for burning

.

Questions to catalogue: *If you weren't yourself that night, who? & if such an amulet cannot exist? Could this domesticate marmot heart ever own another?*

.

Answering machine's a Cuban bolero. Voices warble, the message clear: *Love* is a very feeble word

.

Hear, the nucleus flips. Knock me with a sword of fish: old loves gone dry

.

Crossing the street there is nothing to look away at

Exhibit.

Exhibit.

Handwritten note, taped to a bathroom mirror. Presumably written by the disillusioned former owner of a missing hand towel. Imagination makes you sick with missing. Something you *know* is there, ...

Exhibit.

O that I have pilfered your precious handtowel!
That I shall feed your handtowel to a diarrheic
Labrador, befoul with the diseased wong of a
leper, wiped with stale breath of a million-year-old
caveman, preserve in the taxidermic body of a
puss-newt, spit on with a rabid mongoose, clean
toejam from a Sasquatch, soak in slug urine, wipe
noses of an extended family of sneezy aardvarks,
sop seawater from an epileptic jellyfish, pop boils
of a sun-stroked orangutan, sponge pens of
flatulent hogs, collect lice from a monkey's navel,
swab spit of a camel halitosis, tourniquet slit
throats of maddened ostriches, clear mucus from a
choking bull & drain spinal fluid from a paralyzed
turkey!

O to violate your relic of cleanliness! That your
sinks be filled with mildew of a thousand
slaughtered chickens! That our drains be clogged
with shedding leg-hair of a skank Wolfman! That
your mirrors never be cleaned: that your sideburns
hang uneven & your eyebrows grow to a solid
crossbar! May our unclean fingernails turn
gangrenous & snuff it! That you should learn the
lugubrious sin of dirt! Futility handtowel! Irksome
handtowel! Bowel handtowel! Babel handtowel!
Handtowel javelina jowl! Indigestion handtowel!
Handtowel turd owl! Handtowel brown yowl!
Colon handtowel! Handtowel mad cow growl!
Moth pile handtowel! Sloth bile handtowel!

The author of this ransom note is, presumably, the thief of aforementioned hand towel(See Exhibit 12). The tone suggests a certain, unnamable grudge by the author against the hand towel's former owner. The increasing irrationality & gratuitous appearance of exclamation points imply a particularly lonely individual. Get it backwards. Old is heartbreak, or did I.

Exhibit.

	DEC 1 5 1997	
DEC 2 9 1991 DEC 1 6 97		DEC 1 0 1999
APR 1 5 1992 MAR 2 5 1999		
MAY 1 3 1992 OCT 2 3 1996		JAN 1 8 2001
JUN 0 7 1992 SEP 1 6		
JUN 1 9 1992		OCT 3 1 2001
MAY 1 5 1994 MAY 0 9 2000		
MAR 1 7 1994		
DEC 0 8 1995		
MAY 1 0 1996		
MAY 1 0 1996		
JUL 2 6 1996		
JUL 1 5 1996		

#47-0108 Peel Off Pressure Sensitive

Kept in back of books. Used to keep accurate record of communication with the ghost of the Hotel. Red dates denote a day that ghosts were seen while eating strawberries. Beyond the interview heard, "Oh I feel so unnecessary, horsefly." Phone rings, the living room shifts again. She couldn't stand, the sight of ringing telephones: if they're working or want a straight answer.

Exhibit.

1 Big Mama Thornton, 1 Tippi
Hedren, 1 Max Headroom, 1
salmonella, 1 Sal Mineo, 1 cobbler, 1
cooper, 1 Percoset, 1 shower, 3 Muscle
Shoals, 1 ghost cyclist, 1 Bhanu, 1
Cleveland, 1 machinist, 1 typist, 2
teepee, 3 triptych, 1 cryptic, 2 cynics, 1
Space Ghost, 2 placards, 3 munich, 1
mimic, no Simics, 2 mystics, 1 cheap
trick, 1 ChapStic, 2 Chappequidics, 1
Bisquick, 1 creatin, 1 break in, 2
Wheat Thins, 2 hard ons, 3 din dins, 2
dadas, 4 mamas, 1 Peter Lorre, 15
Edward Goreys, 2 Chaucers, 3
mincers, 1 dicer, 2 dancers, 1 pincher,
2 swingers, 1 tiger, 1 singer, 1 smaller,
2 bigger, 2 ostrich, 1 hostage, 1
possum, 1 supper, 1 sitter, 3 sisters, 1
Digger, 1 sinner, 2 users, 1 winner, 2
Wieners, 1 Weimar, 1 loser, 1 ewe, no
yous, 1 hand towel

Date unknown. Found posthumously on the hotel veranda among the old woman's papers and
seeds. Slipping in and out, these voices; I'd rather be collecting. An instrument, resemblances
of lung, walls & turn in breath. & what other shapes memory takes: the latticed violet-orange of
the afternoon sky – third thing – submission – Kuleshov's dream.

An Answer to Your Ransom Note

"This is what happens, Larry.
This is what happens when you
F(ind) a stranger in the A(lps)."
     —   *Big Lebowski, edited for TV*

Let Z equal A, let B equal Y
Let X equal C and D equal W
Let V equal E, let F equal U

Let T equal G and H equal S
Let R equal I, let J equal Q
Let P equal K and Le equal O

Let N equal . M. Let's meet
then. Two strangers in the middle
Of the Alps. I object

to objectifications of objects
equal to lateral mortifications. Let you
equal I not equal I and I not equal U

Let U not equal you and not I
I equal U equal I equal
You equal I equal U equal I

Out walking this morning as an old trunk bumped through the neighborhood, hauling rolled-up strips of carpet – filled to the brim with them. Sure, they were harmlessly coiled, but still, I couldn't help but associate; one can never help but associate the worst attributes to one's neighbors or an ordinary morning. Come on, when you live down the road from someone who's on the Chamber – when you've seen how trim they keep their lawn – even you, who stays out of such matters, must notice what they've been up to, the after-hours orders to pour tons of manure into unsuspecting citizen's driveways in effort to alleviate the traffic problem. One's bound to suspicion, on early walks, to imagine the self into the role of the broken-legged, secular detective, setting up trip-wire about the yard, hurling mayonnaise on the mailman from the crab apple tree you've been perched in since Tuesday. Aren't you even the least bit curious where they get their horses? one's bound to start calling and hanging up on random numbers picked from the phone book, at least for the briefest gage of public opinion, scanning each tone of the stranger's "Hello..." for a hint of weariness, like-suspicion, or obliviousness. An imprecise system, I know, but I've been noticing distinct patterns to the way they've been catching on their double-l's – perhaps it's this connection. But you must grant one *that*, given the dire circumstances, one's obliged to take matters, certain possibilities, at least staying open to them, well, at least consider blowing the whole town to shit. The whole thing, yes, the ragged wild wolf-children in the moors and all – I don't like it any more than you do, I'm a taxpayer, too. I've considered the dip in property values, and I wouldn't want to put a jinx on the high school football team's undefeated season, not when they're this close to being State Champs – incidentally, wouldn't the Chamber love, just love, that – but just imagine, the beautiful damage we might do together, all the pretty holes in those lovely blue uniforms, that smoky dung scent rolling out across the Tri-State valley. All those dump gulls, stranded up there, swirling in reverse, without land to land their shadows.

Mole seeks mule for meal of eel & ale.

Let's Loch Ness. Not too taut to talk of woks &
Bach. You: no Yaley bull, a mule, or gull. Me:
an eel, or wren's descending trills. Will call an
eel an eel if need feel well. All is fair in eel &
ale. Let's oil an acre with bumble bees. Let's
worship the plumber. Let's whale. Let's mule.
Let's met for mastodon from musk til drawn.
Or prawns are gone. With ants, let's canter
through amber sands. Let an ass mate a mule &
mole. Let's make Seminole, or knot tails of
mule & eel. Let's mastodon, meet an elk in
milk. Let's lick a clock & ask a stag to toast.
Let's whale until Tim calls & all the ale's an
orange peel. Until all is air under the neon "R".
I'll meet you there. I'll eel if you'll mule. Let's
face it: all immoral meals are mortal morsels:
eels & mules, moles & ales. & oats. Germ seeks
worm in Tim to jam twice weekly, to ail on own
terms. Must own bus, or mule. Must aspire to
own acoustic eel. If griffin's gruff, or lust is lost,
must own puffin. Must be active, hold octaves
captive with arachnids. Grackle/grackle-
pterodactyl (preferable). Let's hatch plans,
harpoon a mule. Tired of flowers? Let's meet
for owl of ire, or ham on ion. Let's flatten &
iron an hour. Let's oil an onion, befoul a house
with pheasants. Must like Brahms. No burns.

You said Waldorf, I said Flagstaff. You,
Falstaff. I said false teeth. Teeth, you said, true.
Catullus, you said: catastrophe. Saxophone?
You said, taxicab! Take me! Migraine, you said
magistrate. Magpie, I said pimento. Filament, I
meant memento. Inventive, you said. Transfers
momentum. Moment vetoes TiVo, you said. I
said vitamin. Mingus, you said, but I asked
Mood Indigo. Minnow, said Mia Farrow. Feral,
you shot arrow. Rival, you said. Valor? I need
Valium. You heard linoleum. I said melon, you
harmonium. Rodent, I said, donut. Donut, you
said Jelly Roll. Jovial? You said Morton. I
asked, tom-tom? You said, toppled. Copied lop-
side. I called Interpol. Politely, you said.
Brownie, you said, bad guy. Badgers.
Liposuction, I said potluck. When I say
tragedy, you say Tarzana. Zoltar? Formica. I
said American. Milk-mustache, you said
Calcutta. A Happening! I said, clapping.
Mapping, you drew black bear. I thought tapir,
sent podiatrist. Diaspora's, you said, a
sporophore. Boo-hoo, I said. Hobo, you said,
SoHo's a no go. Oboe, I said, Los Lobos. Over
you said. I heard Omar. Sharif's – you said –
Finnish! Bianca said Britannica. In bicarbonate
I said, solo.

Exhibit. "Idaho Puzzle Piece"
for Bob Roley

A call to the Crossword Crisis Hotline...

provides an answer to the clue that had been troubling: two across is fiddlers! But fiddlers turns what I thought was gossip to rumors. Rumors turns Persia to Serbia. Leer becomes ogle. Ogle turns folders to dossier. Dossier changes slant, slant becomes giant. Giant turns Texans to sexist, sexist turns rung into hunt, and hunt turns Astros to Oilers. Oilers changes language. Language becomes suitcase, tastes become closer that turns apses to Pepsi, egos to eggs; eggs affects grief making growth. Plants becomes ghosts, vote becomes hate, hate changes stymied to tantric. Season must be dissolve, dissolve turns slide into coast. Coast makes leased demise. Demise makes steer meat. Meat makes uselessly hopefully. Hopefully, turns turn into *lafg*, so I get up to get a glass of water, but the sink turns to a tank, the faucet a turret. The turret turns fixtures into dentures, the light becomes glass. A mug turns into a bat, the stove becomes votive, utensils turn to driftwood where a paper-ripped hole of the air swallows toward what a swimming head becomes...

Exhibit. "Little yellow magnet O"

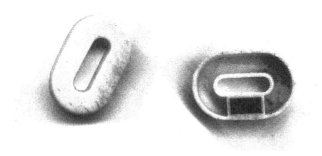

depolarized retractable moon, slung low as an ear, you fold back
the sea to sop glue upon what love-wheels, the wind in opposite
pull, slows our sound, unravels like a client, dark white petal-scent—

love's immutable equation, a tooth mark's sensual for our shard
air, raw fleshly mounds buzzing the chests. Six crisp clefs. Two
visible breaths—

our opal mouth a series of slide projectors, plastic
hearts red-black slivers roaring the moments along—

arkless night, what do you carry to your ethereal shores? Beware
the looping pulls that loom above the salted corpses! Shall we
dissolve to such a size that our places saved with jackstraws—

little yellow magnet o, haul us on to brush the Soutine vague
landscapes with the imbalance of these meltable objects—
moths, dolls, spools of old blood—into your unfathomable yet
obscenely round felt shores, sunken, irretrievable, yet traceable;
fleshly in tow, honey for the unborn—

Exhibit.

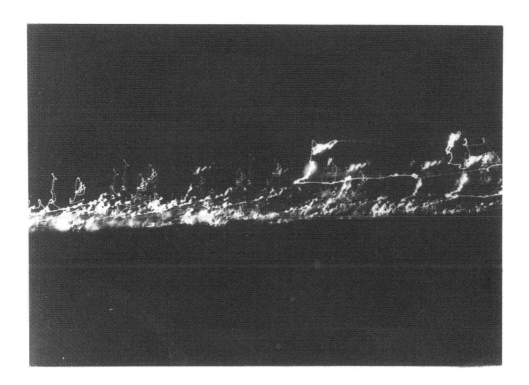

A pier

where I wait in the air for my hair to appear. Out there against costly sprayed waves I spot an upright mare tied to the pier. For fear, the tide's to appear! Where the mare I spy is dry with despair. Who Left you there, mare, to produce such a tear? Bareheaded, I go there, "I'll try to untie!" but a wave unknots me from slats of the stairs by the upright mare who is tied of the pier. As I near the end of the pier it appears the mare's – after all – a mere gag of pears, and me thinks its what the people want to hear it a mare tied to a pier for fear the tide to appear. Let it produce such a tear in the tear in these clothes that one wears. Here, I lament to admit: I ate the horse.

Exhibit. "Your Receipt."

Boston-to-Phoenix watching baseball on seat-back screen batting off turbulence – viewed from without – the plane hitting nose-first onto third base. Luggage on the mound, to watch your own death live on television: the head, a burning globe.

Or: to read the unauthorized tell all of your own disappearance. The ghostwriter's inventions have become fact: you've never owned a red shirt, but last seen wearing one at a Texaco filling station just east of Albuquerque. You've never been to Albuquerque. This becomes false: this is your receipt.

Exhibit.

Wasn't it fun, though? A whole gallop among us. A troupe of vermillion filling in for vaudevillians at a backyard party one July evening. There was Groucho and Zeppo and Chico. You played Harpo. No, I played Buster with lingering fingers in various custards. When lightning struck – nobody seemed to care – you stuck your head in the Tupperware, playing "who's the blindest?" Then we ran home to bed while you clipped out your art. Don't listen to Scientist Lovelock: we live more than one. Harpo, wasn't it fun, though?

Exhibit.

Explanations why I might be missing in or among the AM train steam.

1. Not rain – snow's news. Anger per torture. Torrid deep parts. Rupturic. Arid boa ark.

2. Nostradamus' loose: hung apart, – or, adept at – parching your itch. In the orchard, bored.

3. No trains, new suns: (Gasps.) "Gap is?" "Sure!" "Departure card?" "Board."

Lobby

Balcony, lit up, many gins richer.

rolling out shapes, blown news
Papers. Old cross, crooked moment.

Obscured dance, chiaroscuro, butterscotch.

A weatherman speaks in
air shocked out of

The eye tires in its foreign city.

A visor of digital blood.
Time is measured in funerals.

The answers I leave behind pattern.

Grass railways swallow stadium light.

Puffy morning faces

whose blue can the air finger please turn.

promises slowly climb a stage.

Handbags

bead.
Knotted trunks wet slop petty stands
sage light stops a path

Old visions fall in the road.

Constant engines strap around town.

Rattling jogs.

Reminds around surroundings,

Flip-flop footsteps stop

Paces spark ripples & quick clasps.

the radios at dusk

Hinges rusting open of her arms

Approaching fall, the ushers directionless.
Looking states "one blush if I remember."

Memory & Xerox: a working network.

Embarrassed indiscretions, gestures

A Flock of White Lanterns Make a White Wave

movements beauty plays
the unseen actress

After corners pack the sun,
relived fugues should turn to
Heat, shoulders, scarce spots hanging.
acing a night tide undivided.

No, never.

Insomnia.

Filming? Eye?
Marriage spontaneously fills in theatres.

Standing street water, dusk stinking, I sunk in an
unanchored chair

Yellow the lit circuses

The body thought different..

A thread sat, not threaded, bent

hurries passage, closer

Camera's security draws a breath.

Lightning, sobriety – never cynical.

Through windows: clouds, roar of machinery.

The lanterns enter the river.

Quarrels suck

threatens, fall away.
Wine settles pointed to impossible laugh-track.

Pastor bursts in dream: wet weed,

Closed, small stones, heat.
"My glass also weeps."

Performance isms concrete.

 "Handle against my hand."
Each new day: a narrow wooden room.

Your predictions never mention
Coverings

words turn
off lights in the half-light.

Sleep is where coagulating distance
forms between break and change.

Countless mistaken sunning grooms
The fear vowed never to return
I hung, I slept. I dreamed

The windowed palace turns intact
roof blows through unlocked
curtains escaping shapes of bodied expectations

A radius closing.

Off-road cloud forms who want "freedoms."
A flash light in occupied distance
Efforts

Deleted Scene from the Video Installation

Peeling back the night soil. A small girl under
the hotel awning. Grips a loosely wrapped coil
of sod. The morning doorman – what little
authority that rakish hat permits! – cannot permit
her entrance.

– Microorganisms.

– Microorganisms?

– Where is your mother?

– In the field.

In the field against thin trees lean the beaten
stars, the shell of a dentist chair, an exoskeleton,
the ghost of Fred Astaire.

Exhibit. *"Nine postcards pinned on a hollow wall beside an east-facing window where sits an old Grundig tuned between stations."*

I/ Another Bird

The reflection
ups a sheath on soil

rain on the silo,
a term of magic   This

perhaps bent
with crushes

stalks under a gray-black
night   restless

frames down the perpetual
hill   arching

II/
seeds around his head
whenever Paul wishes snow

his cow clicks eyes
from the brickyard

northing to wake but the rain
sparrows

anesthetics you quickly

the hour immediate
following the sea was different

III/
along the papered
halls, vacant shoes

waits softly for next
thought to

spring "it is
so warm

in here" feels
so, there-

fore, must be

IV/
William Carlos
Williams, it was really nothing

which is to say I've stolen
Paterson from

on twenty-eighth
just as it was   Unread

no one seems to

mind do you   Jack didn't
when I thieved   Arguing...

V/
so that & an and
which birds them

together   Comes to
familiarize with

pauses &
yes   Some notebooks to cat
whose back
ground knows none other

ground   Landing,
an actual bird

VI/
chases a cat down
the throat in

your hair
a crow's tangle

the ceiling a kind
of gonged   racket

dull metal oracles
transit & receipt

opinions wrapped
in fish   Phlegms out

a hand surrounding
materials challenging

VII/
grackle in
your hair
took nothing
but *mauf*
in its throat
a dime

VIII/
nine dimes in the palm

one less than one

Eisenhower etc etc

who loves you > nine

IX/
beginning with something
you said   *You're too*

busy writing down what

I'm saying to hear

what I'm actually
saying

fails a grasp speaks
of the want for you to

answer the fragment
of this junction

without knowing
you would be in-

between to follow your sound
your horses   Your funk

& wagnall's dryness   what silence:
a thousand monk's bones

Ornithology, or
Five Variations on a Sculpture in the Restroom Corridor, or
Nude at the Breakfast Table.

1

Not nude, copper. Stripped
finish. Not blue, a few
yellow feathers. Under
the chair, mysterious
reproduction of eggs
to capture echoes. Blue
is not blue.

2

In blue feathers, blue is
not blue. Blue is
interference. Tiny bubbles.
Difference
in distance of light.

3

The old Grundig mostly tuned between stations in a
north-facing window obscures the harbor where sailors
unload Telefunkens from a dreadnaught. A dry delay of
static. In blue feathers blue is interference. Distance in
difference.

4

Approaching an entrance & on each step a dead bird laid
in gradations of decay. Max Ernst's skeleton parlor;
mamo with a few yellow feathers; tanager-of-seven-
colors; embalmed black woodpecker. Rushing to
retrieve forgotten glasses I saw bones grow feathers.

5

Furthest from one & a numbness
        of growing
        numbers. Positive
afterimage: a humming-
        birdshadow. (Part of
a larger pattern.) From a source
        material, approaching.

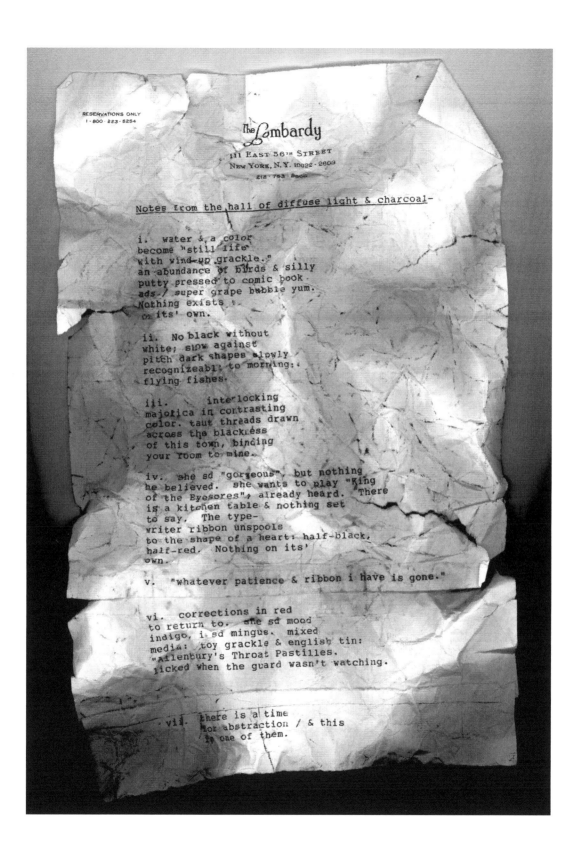

Headphones to ears, a rare cool air Zuks a Midtown. No music: this mix-tape fails, unspools a foot. A few woofs found on our roof though, & a constant pace of hooves. Wolf or wolves – a few? Now a few moans. Such a mournful wail! Hoot's too new to shoot with bow of fir. You howl
while I un-   wound this magnetic wound. A   full mouth of
fallow wool   How howl thou, wolf – flow ?   Moon's foul
red; an eye.   woof song to track a night th-   rough with fur
while I hold   defunct tunes of Lemmy's ear. O   rough fang face
new moves from Moor to fire escapes. Ah! This tape for you's a – Night in Fur – ribbon now, curls four bows. How to play? Fallen down, where hide thy silver; hide where, wolf? O o o – wow – metric symmetry must crave a blurred white sphere or goat on faraway hill. Look down an alley: shallows a hairy shadow. Play out, wolf, for us while this tape won't. Thy bully

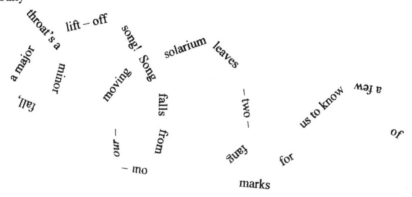

Museum of Thrown Objects: Catalogue of Withdrawals

with Notes from the Curator

"Escher's Trance" (mixed media installation, 3' x 3', metal ensnares, burl oak, mirror glass & glue)

One can never be too wise to the one or two ways out of here…

"Egg of Bridges." (Hand drawn performance piece notes)

"We can describe the relations between things in the world. Some of the things in the world are pictures or signs, while other things are things pictured or signified. For example, the sign saying, '400 meters to the beach' is actually 577 meters to the nearest bit of sand. The picture of the hotel in the holiday brochure was taken on one of the few days that the builders were not working on the ground floor extension and the swimming pool." (Klempner on Wittgenstein)

"The Anxious Subjugate" (11' x 63', motor oil on driftwood)

"When the starry sky, a vista of open seas, or a stained-glass window shedding purple beams fascinate me, there is a cluster of meaning, of colors, of words, of caresses, there are light touches, scents, sighs, cadences that arise, shroud me, carry me away, and sweep me beyond the things I see, hear, or think, The "sublime" object dissolves in the raptures of a bottomless memory. It is such a memory, which, from stopping point to stopping point, remembrance to remembrance, love to love, transfers that object to the refulgent point of the dazzlement in which I stray in order to be.'" (Kristeva)

"aquatint, dry-point, photogravure, spitbite, lithography, silkscreen, embossing, tattoo machine engraving, laser-cutting, collage, crystals, felt paper, enamel, glitter, gold-leaf, gouache, graphite, oil, plasticine" (25' x 12', oil and acrylic on canvas)

Waited three hours, the only to appear: a mistaken identity. A coat-hanger skeleton. The "I" from "we".

"(untitled)", (45' x 6'', celluloid. Last two silent minutes of film. Single shot: snaking line of ticket buyers wrapped steadily around the concert hall –)

"[O]ne sees the loosening of the embrace, apparently so tight, of words and things, and the emergence of a group of rules proper to discursive practice. 'Words and things' is the entirely serious title of a problem; it is

the ironic title of a work that modifies its own form, displaces its own data, and reveals, at the end of the day, a quite different task. A task that consists of not – of no longer – treating discourses as groups of signs (signifying elements referring to contents or representations) but as practices that systematically form the objects of which they speak. (Foucault)

"Private properties " (4.5' x 2', mixed media installation: Eight black pawn stencils, USPS mailbox.)

"The external object occasions a modified and diminished form of sentient suffering (fear), in order to allow the object to be acted upon, in order to prevent the more extreme form of sentient suffering (physical pain). Fear-and-object can thus itself be understood as a partially objectified, hence halfway eliminated, form of pain." (Scarry)

"Afghanistan: an Occupation" (mixed media installation, Billiard table in an interrogation room.)

"Naming suffering, exalting it, dissecting it into its smallest components – that is doubtless a way to curb mourning." (Kristeva)

How the lamplight spins across a room off the rotary telephone.

A mist: indignant host, an almost innocence. Become recognizable, stranger...

Exhibit.
The Irregular Division of Planes or, Water and a Color Contends

1 Perhaps

something in
it has a

rump,
two wings or

fins, perhaps
a bind, or

fist – thus probably
scales, then

feathers the weight-
less tear

2 Discovery of ants

in a glade: embryonic
vegetables, hexagonal

privets & a mule
vibration – two

knotted leaves, unless
fallen
bound to
the concept of stem & stalk –

fish are air & in
respect to birds, landing
is a kind
of answer to

3 Function of background

A Valkyrie fog & the molecules in
charge – : a lop-
sided heart contends

With leaks to dis-
solve completely

A means
of separation –

Static is movable, a

Frequent loss of
frequency asks – in that

Way one speaks
about silence – what

Would you allow to fall

Exhibit. "Litter?"

Dear Litter,
you are so much better than you
think or we think, bitter
you are, obliterated
we think we're better later with-
out you, it is not
better later after
bitter litanies of late
letters. O obituaries!
O better-late-than-nevers!
O custom filters!
Night knits its letter and I
I am better than bitter
but litter, big or
littler, you obliterate better
than any letter. What, bitter?
Better? What, litter?
What's later without you?

Auk Book

There is no mystery surrounding the extinction of these birds: they simply yielded to the inevitable law of the survival of the fittest. through disuse the wings became unfit for service, and the parents could not reach a place of safety for their eggs; and though expert divers, and strong, swift simmers, their legs were almost useless when upon land, and the birds were continually surprised by hunters and captured in large numbers, until the last one perished.

—   Thomas Nutall, 1834.
quoted in "The Rarest of the Rare"

If there is a healing presence of passing strangers – and I believe there is – then, let us never have met. Let the lines be redrawn sharp & short as might any last underwater breath. Might. Or, as written on the verdant dream of the sky: silhouettes of castaway gulls: "Let's go to bed for all the dead ones..." "– and everything else the dead can't do."

Take this origami gull. A paper cut's more dangerous than a haunting. Even the thinnest slice is enough for invasion. So many collapsible chambers. Best to remain moveable, shifting, than propped up with a rock in feathered wind. Never prepared for the worst: the hinges rusting shut, a possibility the gulls will not return from their sea migration. The possibility of complete collapse.

Neighbors came knocking to inform
"Your house is on fire"
Too busy acting
Like children while playing to answer
The cloud offers its cup,
A lean key, scabby heart
By the time I get my pants on
You're gone

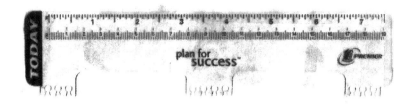

Plan for Success: seven
inches? Sad future.
Let me measure this rate of success – chance
we'll sleep again – with measurements of fallen
hair.
At least, more expendable than inches. This rate of falling:
bald & nude in no time. Image not to scale, weighs
heavier. Let me borrow this seagull, Jack.
It's self already borrowed? Good
Christ. Never borrow from the dead,
death is only a migration. The dead
always return to take much, much more.

Frequently I lose myself in this hedge
Maze, these celluloid stairs cannot show
Me the way. Couldn't hear you clear
Before. Now, loud. Keep soft side tuned
Low. I can never hear the finger point
Imprinted upon these implications.
(As if it were someone else's fault.)
Knifeless
We gush at mere contact.
This shared air

11: EAST 56 TH STREET
NEW YORK, N. Y. 10022-2603

Begin the sequence of sending & talking
with yourself. Sending these dead letters
back, the seagulls back, turn black
passing through smoke of your burning
house.
Cloud shadows of
              cows
on the killing floor. Don't fool yourself:
the voices said your character isn't
distinct enough to become historical.
Best to marionette, throw yourself
beneath the great meat wheel.
But all I could find on that sad hill
a sly gull
a single doll
a double-parked taxi

Lost in these echoless cells, we can't hear
our own. The sounds we make cannot
comprehend their loss. What is missing.
Doesn't know what it's missing
Exists. But to know is much,
much worse. Bliss, something I cannot
ignore. Laughed until coughed.
Something horrible in the lungs
leaked from these seams of same
collapsed chambers. Me —
thinking they were air
tight

Dear Jen

OFF to L.A. for the weekend.
Another wedding in L.A. It seems
getting a screenplay is a necessity for these
weddings alone. Another, my sister & Dan's
is in May.
Rilke came in the mail last
week. Thanks. I have written a better
poem for you. A last tinkering,
as usual.
Had an epiphany last week talking
(arguing) w/ my dear overbearing
friend Gary. Will write you a better letter
later. got a

When everyone's gone home to the factories, I sneak into the dead
Letter office to answer the unanswerables. "Dear Anne,
Feeling great!" Try not to look at it this way:
To answer is to create
Another death. The most creative act
Is not to answer. Anne,
You will never know. I will never know
You. The universe
Ends with a ringing telephone

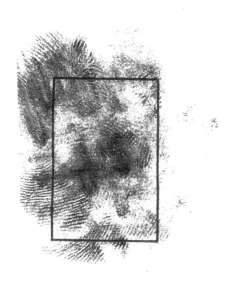

Beneath glass flowers, obscured by kid finger's
leavings
the most important work of art
you will never see. Leaving,
the museum will ask you to return your eyes;
such visions cannot escape
these cells. Imagine the migrations
to their nations of origin. Imagine the bookings
at the Lombardy Hotel. Imagine the lines.
The most beautiful work of art
Obscures
A most beautiful work

Dear Jen

OFF to L.A. for the weekend. Another wedding in L.A. At some point selling a screenplay is a necessity for these weddings alone, another, my sister & Dan's is in May.

Rilke came in the mail last week. Thanks. Have written a another poem for you. A last tinkering, as usual.

Had an epiphany last week talking (arguing) w/ my dear overbearing friend Gary. Will write you a better letter later. got a

Dear Anne,
I should never know you as real, if you received this, receive anything. They keep
the receipts from me. You will never know I sleep in the dead letter office. And quite a stamp on my forehead: This page is intentionally BLANK. Because: (a) Four more years; (b) I love you; and (c) There's a ghost in the John. I've been holding this in four days: Dear Anne,
you never existed, bud down on Rose Bay by the sugar-glass plants. I can taste you in this. But you never existed, rather never exited these hollow cells. A better letter later ... Please let these letters drop
pit by bit. How can you catch them
With this
Gull in the mouth

Dear Anne,
Glad to see you're finally able to give
(what you always said you would)
Give your shadow the slip
Deliver me, please,
These letters to places you've never let
A room within the book – is not a darkened
cell. This delivery is
Not a sentence

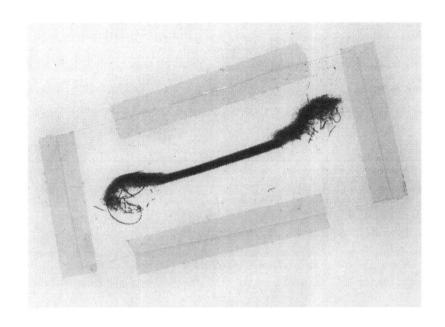

Couldn't hear though this time
Place this in your ear & there you are
Still in bed, discussing stage directions
"bed-left, bed-right" (depends
whether standing or lying) who's
our audience? The ceiling, the gulls, the
ghosts. "Let's go to bed..."
                    No,
I don't want to be a pornographic ghost film.
Too late. The shadow has already stripped
Itself from your body, Without a self
there is no shadow
Self. The inverse also true

RHODODENDRON MAXIMUM LINN.

The Rose Bay Rhododendron, modeled in glass, is a hardy species native from Nova
Scotia to Georgia and is widely cultivated

MODEL 608   R. BLASCHKA, 1890

Who would have guessed this glass
Shallow
Enough to contain multitudes
Guilt, flightless wonder. Feathered
Ponderousness. Spills
The sea knows best. A better letter
Later bellows its bitter tastes against our shores.
Nudges its edge along slowly as if
We – forgetting our bird's eyes – can't
Notice such intrusion. It's just that we try
So hard. Fail
Every evening to stay awake until morning.
Guiding its ships in-
                    Stead
Guarding the vacancy
Our laid awake songs

My, how the mind grates. Migrates. The seagulls head out to sea
to finish what they started. Re-
turning to shit on the flotsam's whiteness.
Meet me in the park by the Sheraton Commander, Cambridge
town is best this time of year: the old men are off their benches,
going older places. Leave it all
to us: we feel like children when playing dead. Gulls
turning, tracing the livestock
patterns. Bellow there, mid-flight
in turn, abandon plans

In constant ascent & descent, the ghosts
of the Lombardy Hotel. On at five, off at three.
Through the wall, misheard "moment"
as "Movement". From the shaft of this unspoken-
of place. Sewn by our choices,
our voices, all the places
they've been

The ear machine replays
"When we leave this place, can we take
Our bodies, leave
Everything else – the gulls, these
Animal shadows. Now light this
Let's go up: the roof in white flame
The white surface
Blank
Petalface

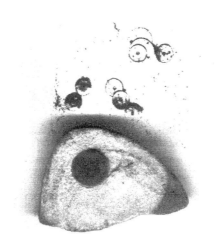

"And are we angels yet, Bird?"
Jack Through disuse the wings unfit for service
The auk is now a rock. Who are you fooling
Rock
You're no *Alca impennis*
Last recorded sighting June 3, 1844
Two birds – possibly a mated pair – clubbed
to death by fishermen –
Mocking bird, rock is not your color!
hidden here as I hide. Non-existent,
non-extinct. So wings cannot be sewn?
Our choices, our voices, all the places
Bacteria in the meteor.
Peridot crystal. Perdido, perdido. Bird? Wrestless
Auk. Can only extinct things return
fat children? Let my angels be the fattest,
so many voices tuned through me

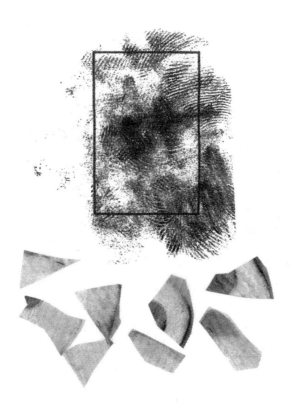

Walking around these wet streets
Out of her rocks
Sin. Gully. Positively gully.
The most beautiful work of art
The one with the magic sequence in her pocket
Sequins
And a rock. Thrown (birdless) through glass flowers. Their edges
Softened in whitepetalflame –
Ignore
The rock passes through. Wingless one – not glass –
In flight
that shatters. Patternless
magic sequence

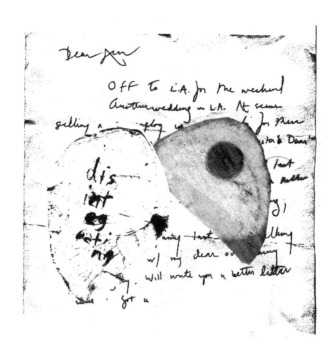

Dear Anne, Bring back the white petals
And the pier. The gulls
Or answer where we have all
Disappeared to. My the mind a flightless
Auk. These better letters belie our extinct
Biologies.
Crush the petal sea to white dye. An outward
exchange the weight of an aukless world. Thoughtlessly evokes the magic
sequins. (All we have left.)
There is no wild gold
Sewn into the world. So why mention
This? Is Precise
                   Ly why
We mention this. The faithless
Faceless rock
Returns. A gully shadow.
Return us to our sea and we will give you back
This faithlessness. Just grant us this

We only go away so we can feel
How we come back again
From a desert wash appears
Infinite shape
Mown in by phantasmagoric dirt bike riders
And from its tired path real flowers bloom
We
Peer upon the edge of eight
And drop a rock (a real
aukless rock) In. To return us.
We re
          A pier
Upon the edge
Of eight

The Edies

"a picture held us captive"
– Wittgenstein

another faced within these clothes – turns
        away – the colors,
dawned and down –   on vacation
        you still have to take your pills – so there
is continuation – within the bodied
        look – before the railing – looks   completes
the gesture to beyond   railing
        at the railed-against sea

            *

how many forgotten plots
do we dream each night –
his smile goofy in its love for hers his arms
legs & lederhosen cross the hollow
        log   in mock eagerness for
her smile as she looks a way, warm
& fleeting one that fills
the afternoon with soft despair
of its direction behind them   a Norwegian
wooded summer sun floods through
on towards its end display

            *

I was just listening
to your "I don't care's"
& now I'm the only one here

on this train because
the other two
are making out,

are somewhere else.
So where did you say
you keep the ice

trays? Back again "and. they.
are. still. HERE."
Laughing

laughing done
like "Like five syllables"
is five syllables

            *

should I be disappointed when I don't expect

an answer? What did it feel like coming
out of the jungle? Is a cactus as cruel
as the grinding cicada? How can the short statue
of dark skin (Mexican?) Jan seem to sweat even
under the shaded ridiculous red
topped sombrero foreground obvious "native"
against your frumped up tourist pose
represent? Do sunglasses help? Why
were you there? Does that angled on sun
mean you'd been at it all day? Were
those the most appropriate slacks? Why
the long faces can patterns of flowers stand
to represent the same or even more
power over say, a floral dressed pattern?
No really why the long   faces

                *

(*Dislocations*)

Is reflecting on the reflected flash in the soon-
to be picture frame as kind
as a songbook lesson how the upper
registers getaway from us bother
us so when at this relative's gold rimmed
desk listening to another room's broad
casts in dislocations and whirlpools
The sources of light in the living
rooms at mid-century midtown, the fragility of blue
plates, gaudiness of stranger dolls, glint
on the watch, tooth and plastic eventual
ominous even if it wasn't just light on a toy
gun, and that would be different than how
unusual how one "learns, continues" despite

                *

Season of the Octopi

Silhouette of that man
Against the evening sea

There is no man only
The shape of man

There is no sea
Only the shape of sea

166

Silhouette of the sea
Against an afternoon

Blue there is no sky
Only the shape of

After silhouettes of
After the shape of it falls

On shoulders of the
Silhouette of no man

Slides into skied sea

   *

chords bone up in my hand. hurdles
imagined crowds fallen by car-light
and fake southern accents stern, of the No
neck monster "Julia!" "Julia, where..."
There are some things in this
(by crutch) *you just have to face*
alone the broad lawn hedged in modern architecture
treeless so gage-less of another atmosphere
garage-less centering go figure
You in ambiguous sunlit green
          sweater
keyed in on edge.
     Shadow faces
      the water wedge
expressionless not even for the halved century
later family calling desperate to know, the
strange tricked widths, your unbeknownst
  skied-in blemishes

   *

little past one fast fades
archaics escape / the eyes want
with the knowing grin page dust
corner mark chewed through
simple over-thoughts curl track
among bric-a-brac of night boxes. Beside the
bed night time light table slides
several cat-in-the-windows self
portraits in ribbed gold mirror (how
many eyes can the eyes count) & the gloved
children yelling down the wall for the uniform

men to throw a free ball
up into the orange night which the crowd
leaning in all directions disappears into

                    *

proud as corsage double worn
Or, "metallic"
the space between them military

                    *

A White Window

                    Trims the blue door caps
the blush tray, the mineral expressions
on the blonde chill dress faces
water
            brushes
            as yet un-cracked
            hard boiled eggs

plate such a blurring exchange
                                        beyond calculating
weeds   uncut   Whomever
        it is should arrive a stranger reprise
                        such a puzzled slope
chins the backyard fences

                    *

Ignoring what keeps as you drive
that red tint into oblivion
Fuck-all to the compasses of ash
            tucked up, near
                        your heated joy   a visor
The lines of your face that keep the sea
parched   without meaning.   Fathoms
                        Dipped shoulders
steer the ignored to a nameless
horizon frames Edith open
hung loosely   back &   to the elements

                    *

Gas trick and flight remembers
the song in vinyl embers
            A cumulous code

damp by rain swat vent trick
Rocks that make up the roof farms
                    snows
                        on liquor barn
they parade you around so as to meet
Everyone   each floods natures, each scene depicts
A future remains of solids like quells
A beach dune seed brush   Uncertain
what you have gotten
                    successfully out of
                    folly

        the name
                    of your hometown –
"old magnet" –
fastens itself to your chest

                    *

Rattle of copper wind hearth plate
gray auto-port low beneath the
high seventies green-style
lit around darkened numbers,
as if an accuracy curates
The laughable temp-
        orary ash as written in
brick by the loud florid flame-crowns

        *

is the name of this stone bang keeper
Tuesday rousts the human crustaceans
Escutcheons outside   of the palace
post-meeting meetings   talk
tilt harmony packaging tints
into idling trunks where someone's left
a camera   behind was no accident
to the half open door package
under crook hats pull
around the hard ear turns
down rain ridges entrance steps
THOMAS HELWYS "touts
est possible dans les chuchotements"
Somewhat   agreeable whispers

        *

"coming in off the water"
        steeped in hungry birds of peppermint
put together pairs of the pear tree puzzle
        remains a sigh besides the sign
                "2/3ds done"

                        *

Some picture takes us captive
Pale wall-like February
Marsh to look back upon approaching
                Sun lines
Guests   (the approach)   decent in
Brilliant Sunday bests   folk song visits
Suppose the house plant and curtain
Near the embraced cuff
Hand and pants toggle   the cameras in
   uneasy retries pose these faces gleam
And pearls and eyes
Set   hair   approaches   needless, pulling
        Taken like static
Aback   a fire pokes its dominance

                        *

Formalism, or the gnats

                Someone like a villain bobs
        along among the mustard seed swabs
the emptiness sparks
                use of words for details   (obvious)
        the person talking in the room
                        listens
        outside the room
                listens
        movements of stress   , the question
                        is of no particular reason
of an accuracy: verb – subject – action
        clear for a while (compliments)

plaid draw strings out of closet / In another storyline a solo
        romanticism   lost along the folds of the estate
                        qualifications appear
                                frail
                                yet influential,

"the engines" erase relations   in satisfactory
                                thoroughness

"to be real and incomplete"
Embody two
    fundamental phases and persons
                        -fications
    the foregone   gropes pulses & symbols
                ferried beyond who

     *

hands a frame the window splattering stars

funny little pointed hats commemorate birth

     *

Last leaves. Scatter
Form. The city tree:
 O a ea e e i a e ee
i forget my hamburger

Andrew K. Peterson is the author of "My Worth" (Black Lodge Press, forthcoming 2010), and collaborated with poet Elizabeth Guthrie on "Between Here and the Telescopes" (Slumgullion, 2008). Recent and forthcoming journal publications include: *Dusie, 350 Poems Project, Fact-Simile's The A sh Anthology,* and */The Offending Adam/*. Received an MFA in Poetry from The Kerouac School at Naropa University. He is a co-founder and editor of Livestock Editions, a collective devoted to publishing experimental poetry. For more information, please visit: thelivestockbarnyard.blogspot.com.

Made in the USA
Charleston, SC
21 November 2013